A

Yorkshire

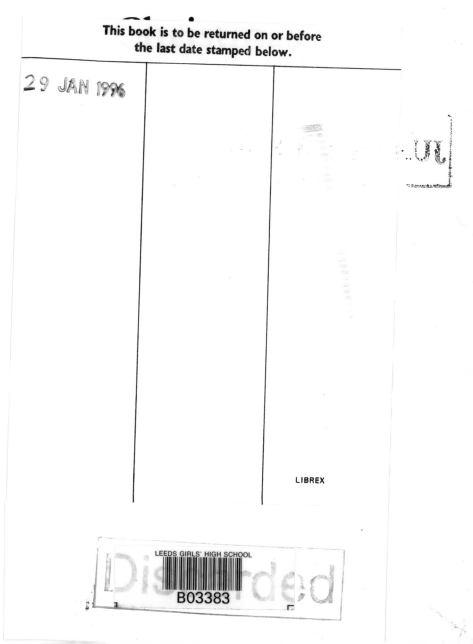

This book is to be returned on or before
the last date stamped below.

29 JAN 1996

LIBREX

ALAN SUTTON PUBLISHING
BRUNSWICK ROAD · GLOUCESTER

ALAN SUTTON PUBLISHING INC.
WOLFEBORO FALLS, NH 03896–0848

First published 1989

British Library Cataloguing in Publication Data

A Yorkshire Christmas.
1. Great Britain. Christmas, history
I. Collard, George
394.2'68282'0941

ISBN 0–86299–639–2

Library of Congress Cataloging in Publication applied for

Cover illustration: Detail from 'Street Musicians' by Brian
Gordon (*Photograph: The Bridgeman Art Library*)

Typesetting and origination by
Alan Sutton Publishing Limited
Printed and bound in Great Britain by
WBC, Bridgend, Mid Glam.

from

The Holly-Tree

CHARLES DICKENS

Dickens, it is believed, used the George and New Inn at Greta Bridge in Yorkshire for this scene in 'The Holly-Tree', en route to the infamous Yorkshire Schools at Bowes.

Christmas Eve

At nine o'clock at night, on a Yorkshire moor, a cheerful burst from our horn and a sound of talking, with a glimmering and moving about of lanterns, roused me from my drowsy state. I found that we were going to change.

They helped me out, and I said to a waiter, whose bare head became as white as King Lear's in a single minute, 'What inn is this?'

'The Holly-Tree, sir,' said he.

'Upon my word, I believe that I must stop here,' said I.

Now the landlord, and landlady, and the hostler, and the post boy, and all the stable authorities, had already asked the coachman if he meant to go on. The coachman had replied, 'Yes'.

I saw my portmanteau got out stiff, like a frozen body, then I followed the landlord, landlady, and waiter of the Holly-Tree upstairs.

3

I thought I had never seen such a large room as that into which they showed me. It had five windows, with dark red curtains that would have absorbed the light of a general illumination; and there were complications of drapery at the top of the curtains, that went wandering about the wall in a most extraordinary manner. I asked for a smaller room and they told me there was no smaller room. They could screen me in, however, the landlord said. They brought a great old japanned screen, with natives (Japanese, I suppose) engaged in a variety of idiotic pursuits all over it, and left me roasting whole before an immense fire.

My bedroom was some quarter of a mile off, up a great staircase at the end of a long gallery; and nobody knows what a misery this is to a bashful man who would rather not meet people on the stairs. It was the grimmest room I have ever had the nightmare in; and all the furniture, from the four posts of the bed to the two old silver candlesticks, was tall, high-shouldered, and spindle-waisted. Below, in my sitting room, if I looked round my screen, the wind rushed at me like a mad bull; if I stuck to my arm-chair, the fire scorched me to the colour of a new brick. The chimney-piece was very high, and there was a bad glass — what I may call a wavy glass — above it, which, when I stood up, just showed me my anterior phrenological developments; and these never looked well, in any subject, cut short off at the eyebrow. If I stood with my back to the fire, a gloomy vault of darkness above and beyond the screen insisted on being looked at; and, in its dim remoteness, the drapery of the ten curtains of the five windows went twisting and creeping about, like a nest of gigantic worms.

When I travel, I never arrive at a place but I immediately want to go away from it. Before I had finished my supper of broiled fowl and mulled port, I had impressed upon the waiter in detail my arrangements for departure in the morning.

Breakfast and bill at eight. Fly at nine. Two horses, or, if needful, even four.

Tired though I was, the night appeared about a week long.

In the morning I found that it was snowing still, that it had snowed all night, and that I was snowed up. Nothing could get out of that spot on the moor, or could come at it, until the road had been cut out by labourers. When they might cut their way to the Holly-Tree, nobody could tell me.

It was now Christmas Eve. Still being snowed up was a thing I had not bargained for. I felt very lonely.

Old Christmas Traditions in Yorkshire

There is magic in the very name of Christmas. Everyone has some happy recollections, though most will say that it isn't what it used to be, and that each Christmas has seen the end of some precious memory. 'Kursmas is nowt like it yance were hereabout!' Dickens said as much over 150 years ago, but when we look further into it we find the tradition more complicated and less subject to change than at first we thought.

Many of the old customs were pagan, but the Venerable

Bede, who is buried in Durham Cathedral in a chapel restored with outstanding beauty and simplicity by George Pace of York, believed that they should be retained and converted 'from the worship of the devils to the service of the true God'.

Bede visited Ripon Cathedral, where his friend Cuthbert's body was to lie before finding its final home in Durham. He also stayed with his friend Chad at Lastingham, near Pickering, and with Egbert, Archbishop of York. Bede recalls that Egbert, who died in 729 AD at the age of ninety, used to fast for forty days before Christmas. He allowed himself 'a scanty ration of bread and skim milk, for he used to keep the previous day's fresh milk in a flask, and having skimmed off the cream the next day he drank what was left with a little bread'.

Well, at least that's one custom that's gone!

The Yule Log

The ceremony of the yule log was introduced to Yorkshire by the Norsemen as they swept down from the North with their naval fleet to land at Scarborough. They burnt oak logs to honour their god, Thor (who gave his name to Thursday), and this coincided with the ancient English tradition of burning a log at the winter solstice to signify warmth and light, a reminder of the undying sun. The Church, however, said the log should be of ash; it was an ash fire the shepherds made in Bethlehem to keep the baby Jesus warm, because only ash burnt without sparks and splutter.

And so the yule log was fetched by young boys pushing and dragging it through the snow. Then it was rolled on to the fire to burn throughout the vigil of the Nativity and Christmas Day, and to smoulder on till Twelfth Night. The ashes were thought to have medicinal properties, especially for the cure of toothache. Sometimes a piece of the yule log, or 'clog' as it was often called, was saved and put under the bed to stay there

Come bring with a noise,
My merry, merry boys,
The Christmas Log to the firing . . .
Robert Herrick

until the following Christmas so as to preserve the house from fire or to quell a raging storm.

In the Dales, to mark the lighting of the yule log on Christmas Eve, church bells were rung and the children gathered in the streets beating drums and blowing trumpets. This was followed by the lighting of the huge Yule Candle, and if the candle went out for any reason it heralded evil and bad luck for the unfortunate household. As the log blazed on the fire, chestnuts were roasted and tales told of the wandering spirits roaming in the dales and on the moors, unable to find rest.

Mistletoe

Mistletoe has always been regarded with suspicion by the Church, either because of the custom of kissing under it or

because of its association with the Druids' fertility rite. The Arch-Druid used to cut the mistletoe from the apple tree in November with a golden sickle and it was caught, as it fell, by virgins holding a white cloth, then distributed and hung over doorways to work healing, protect against witchcraft and bring fertility to the land and people. The Church forbade its use in places of worship with one exception – York Minster. There, each Christmas, it was laid on the altar by the clergy, and 'a public liberty, pardon and freedom to all sorts of inferior and wicked people at the gates of the city to the four corners of the earth' was proclaimed.

Large bunches of mistletoe for sale in the markets at Christmas are proof that it still enjoys a traditional role, even if that role is somewhat changed. When, a hundred years ago, people were asked for their views about it, a typical reply was:

A delicate question i' faith. Under the circumstances we think you would be justified in kissing all good young men who may visit your house this Christmas if you can lure them under the fatal branch,

or

He who will not when he may
When he will he shall have 'nay'.

Christmas presents

Santa Claus, or St Nicholas, as the patron saint of boys and girls, was remembered in giving children gingerbread or toys, but this was on 6 December. It was the Americans who invented 'Father Christmas' in the nineteenth century, dressed him up in his red robes, white hair and whiskers, and set the commercial enterprise alight – the one we now know. But that is *not* Yorkshire. What does derive from Yorkshire goes back to

the time when Severus, Emperor of Rome, lived and reigned in York for three years *c.* 200 AD. High-ranking officials were expected to present gifts to the Emperor on the festival of Kalends, which coincided with Christmas. These gifts were usually presents of cake and honey representing sweetness and gold, but later they became more elaborate as the greed of the Emperor increased!

> *Christmas was always a time of feasting and merry-making, but Nancy and Ernest Tindall of Pickering recall that for them it was made special by those lovely customs of the North Riding such as 'Lucky Birds', 'Waits', and the eating of Frumenty or Fluffin, Sledmere gingerbread with cheese, and Pepper Cake.*

Lucky Birds

Lucky Birds were small boys and girls, well muffled against the cold wind that blows in the North Riding, who went from house to house in the towns and villages, knocking on doors and calling out,

> I wish you a Merry Christmas and a Happy New Year.
> Please may I be the lucky bird here!

Similarly, on New Year's morning, the children, but this time the girls alone, went knocking on doors and calling out,

> I wish you health and strength and a Happy New Year.
> Please may I be the lucky bird here!

On each occasion the lucky birds were rewarded with a small amount of money. Very few children do this nowadays, but around Pickering some still do.

9

Waits

Waits, the watchmen of the village or town, were another tradition over the twelve days of Christmas. Groups of men would go out after midnight, no doubt having been sustained in the local hostelry till then, calling out,

> Good morning Mr and Mrs Smith and all the rest of the family. It's one o'clock on a fine night!

Then on to the next house, and so on. And it always *was* a fine night, as far as Ernest can recall – but perhaps they only went out on fine nights. The Waits were certainly famous everywhere, especially in Leeds, where they had an impressive badge of office in the form of an oval plaque of silver.

Sword Dancers and other Seasonal Activities

Sword dancers were rather more obscure, and perhaps confined to certain areas such as Pickering and Hansworth near Sheffield. They were called 'Font Pleaves' – no one seems to know how to spell it, but that's the way it is pronounced. They used to go around like Morris Dancers to the villages at Christmas time. Goathland still has something similar called The Dancing Plough Stots.

Carols are still sung in period costume in the Castle Museum, York; in Ripon there has always been a Mummers' play on the streets on Boxing Day, and there are a number of Hunts (for example, the Badsworth).

Frumenty, Frumentie, Frumity or Fluffin

Returning to the Christmas treats, it would not be Christmas without Frumenty or Fluffin. Frumenty was a famous sort of spiced porridge made from corn (the name comes from the

The Wait's Badge

Pork pies for Christmas. Pork butchers, Francis Hatfield & Son, Hallgate, Cottingham, 1909. Hatfield's pies and sausages were very well known in the district

Brass ash-tray – a Christmas gift from Francis Hatfield & Son, Pork Butchers, Cottingham

Latin *frumentum*, meaning corn). It was very popular in the Dales and around Filey, where it was taken on Christmas Eve along with Wensleydale cheese and gingerbread, for which Sledmere was famous. The secret of the Frumenty was in the recipe:

> Simmer a quantity of kibbled wheat [kibbled means ground smooth in a mortar] in water for 12 hours, then add a nut of butter, some cinnamon, nutmeg or mixed spice, currants and sugar. Serve hot, with cream and RUM.

Fluffin was the same, except that barley was used instead of wheat. 'In the past we in the north never suffered so much in times of famine,' Nancy says, 'as we always ate more porridge than wheat bread. Lots of people we know always have it in winter – as we do.'

Frumenty was sometimes supplemented and enriched, to give rise to 'Christmas' or 'plum' pudding.

Gingerbread, fruit cakes and loaves, and apple pie were all eaten with cheese, hence the saying,

> An apple pie without cheese is like a kiss without a squeeze.

In East and West Ayton, near Scarborough, and I believe in other parts of the North Riding, a sort of parkin was made at Christmas called Pepper Cake, or Carol-Singing Cake. Nancy remembers children going round the houses singing the rhyme,

> A little bit of pepper cake
> A little bit of cheese,
> A cup of cold water
> And a penny if you please.

13

How long ago this died out she doesn't know – perhaps it still goes on somewhere – but the recipe hasn't disappeared, and many people make it at Christmas.

$1\frac{1}{2}$ lb plain flour $1\frac{1}{2}$ lb black treacle
$\frac{1}{2}$ lb butter   4 eggs (beaten)
$\frac{1}{2}$ lb soft dark brown sugar   1 teaspoon bicarbonate of soda
1 oz ground cloves   Milk

Rub the butter into the flour, stir in the sugar and cloves, then add the treacle, eggs, and bicarbonate of soda mixed with a little milk. Pour the mixture into a large, well-greased tin, and bake at 170 °C for $1\frac{3}{4}$ hours.

Yorkshire Christmas Pie

Pies have always been extremely popular fare, but none more so than Christmas Pie. This recipe has been traditional in

A Yorkshire Christmas Pie, from C.F. Francatelli's *Modern Cook* of 1855

Yorkshire for hundreds of years. The main ingredient was goose – always one of the main dishes at Christmas. The goose, and other poultry such as turkey, chicken, and small game birds, were completely boned, the smallest bird wrapped within the next largest, and so on until a substantial mass of meat had been built up, the corners being filled up with forcemeat and hardboiled eggs. The meat was well seasoned with mace, pepper, salt and nutmeg. The whole was then enclosed in a pastry crust and baked in a slow oven for about four hours. When the pie was cooked and cooled, a hole was made in the lid, and gravy or clarified butter poured in.

The pastry was not intended to be eaten – it was just a container and, as these pies were often sent to friends and relatives as presents, had to be strong enough to withstand a journey, possibly as far away as London. The pie was served cold, cut into wedges, with plenty of pickles as well as spiced orange rings, pickled pears or spiced prunes.

Dickens Christmas Festival at Malton

There are Dickensian Christmas festivals held all over Yorkshire, especially in Grassington, Haworth, Helmsley and Malton. The oldest and best documented is held in Malton and Norton. Here the Dickens Festival takes place, amid crinolines and period costume, in the week before

· A Yorkshire Christmas ·

Christmas, with street fayres, horse-drawn carriages, carols and music supplied by costumed buskers in the streets and pubs. Malton Library features a special Dickens exhibition, and Malton Museum displays, for instance, an 'intriguing collection of Victorian underwear and oddities'. There are competitions galore – Fagin's Pickings, Victorian Costume, Christmas Food, Horse and Rider, and so on.

So what is the connection between Dickens, Christmas and Malton? The great author is said to have written much of A Christmas Carol *during his many visits to Easthorpe Hall near Malton, the home of his close friend, Charles Smithson. A solicitor, Smithson had an office in the town which is believed to have been the model for Scrooge's establishment.*

Once upon a time – of all the good days in the year, on Christmas Eve – old Scrooge sat busy in his counting-house. It was cold, bleak, biting weather: foggy withal: and he could hear the people in the court outside go wheezing up and down, beating their hands upon their breasts, and stamping their feet upon the pavement-stones to warm them. The City clocks had only just gone three, but it was quite dark already: it had not been light all day: and candles were flaring in the windows of the neighbouring offices, like ruddy smears upon the palpable brown air. The fog came pouring in at every chink and keyhole, and was so dense without, that although the court was of the narrowest, the houses opposite were mere phantoms. To see the dingy cloud come drooping down, obscuring everything, one might have thought that Nature lived hard by, and was brewing on a large scale.

The door of Scrooge's counting-house was open that he might keep his eye upon his clerk, who in a dismal little cell beyond, a sort of tank, was copying letters. Scrooge had a very small fire, but the clerk's fire was so very much smaller

that it looked like one coal. But he couldn't replenish it, for Scrooge kept the coal-box in his own room; and so surely as the clerk came in with the shovel, the master predicted that it would be necessary for them to part. Wherefore the clerk put on his white comforter, and tried to warm himself at the candle; in which effort, not being a man of a strong imagination, he failed.

'A merry Christmas, uncle! God save you!' cried a cheerful voice. It was the voice of Scrooge's nephew, who came upon him so quickly that this was the first intimation he had of his approach.

'Bah!' said Scrooge, 'Humbug!'

The *Yorkshire Gazette* of 10 February 1912 records:

Dickens first visited Malton in 1843, at which time Mr Smithson was living at Easthorpe Manor, now occupied by the Hon. Francis Dawnay. It is said that when the novelist arrived by the York coach at the Talbot Hotel, there was not available any proper conveyance in which he could proceed to Easthorpe. He was told, however, that there was a hearse, and without further ado Dickens chartered this unusual vehicle and travelled to Easthorpe alongside the driver on the box! While at Easthorpe Dickens began to 'draw' the character of 'Sairey Gamp', and probably wrote part of *Martin Chuzzlewit*, in which that estimable female appeared. Dickens also wrote, while at Malton, a poem entitled 'A Word in Season' for an annual edited by Lady Blessington. The poem is given in full in Forster's *Life of Dickens*.

At this time, too, Dickens' younger brother, Alfred Lamert, was living at Malton. He was the engineer employed in connection with the construction of the York and Scarborough, and Malton and Driffield lines of railway and probably resided there for nearly ten years. He lodged for

some time at Hillside Cottage, Greengate (now occupied by the widow of a nephew of Mr Charles Smithson), and afterwards went to reside at Derwent Cottage, Scarborough Road.

When Dickens next visited Malton it was to attend the funeral of Mr Smithson, who died in April 1844. Mr Smithson had a few months before left Easthorpe Manor, and taken up his residence at the Abbey, Old Malton, and it was here that he died. He was buried in the churchyard at Old Malton. With members or connections of Mr Smithson's family, Dickens' intercourse long continued, but there is no record of any further visits to Malton. The late Mr R.J. Smithson, who was once jocularly told by Dickens that he was the prototype of the fat boy in *Pickwick*, was a nephew of Mr Charles Smithson, and one of the last acts of his life was to recount to a local gathering his reminiscences of the novelist's visits to Malton.

On one occasion, when Dickens visited the town, he was brought into contact with a Mrs Jump who lived in the low white house still standing in its own grounds in Middlecave. Mr Jump, who, with his wife, is still remembered by a few local people, was head clerk in a Malton lawyer's office, and it is suggested that it is through his occupation that Dickens became acquainted with the couple. Mrs Jump is described as an odd character, who wore old-fashioned ringlets – a description which does not altogether coincide with Mrs MacStinger, in which character she appears in *Dombey and Son*. Presumably Mrs Jump did not make a very good impression on Dickens, as we are introduced to Mrs MacStinger as a widow and a termagent, who made the life of her lodger, Captain Cuttle, a perpetual misery. One of her idosyncracies was to chastize her son Alexander very liberally, and then seat him on a paving-stone to cool!

Traditional Yorkshire Carol

The tune for the verse is almost identical to another which was often sung in the streets of Leeds in the 1850s. About 1910, the Revd J.T. Horton of Bradford reported that the Leeds tune was still sung by the Waits in the West Riding.

· *A Yorkshire Christmas* ·

We've been awhile a-wandering
Amongst the leaves so green,
But now we come a-wassailing,
So plainly to be seen . . .

For it's Christmas time,
When we travel far and near;
May God bless you and send you
A happy New Year.

We are not daily beggars
That beg from door to door;
We are your neighbours' children
For we've been here before . . .

We've got a little purse,
Made of leathern ratchin skin;
We want a little of your money
To line it well within . . .

Bring us out a table
And spread it with a cloth,
Bring us out a mouldy cheese
And some of your Christmas loaf . . .

Good master and good mistress,
While you're sitting by the fire,
Pray think of us poor children
That's wandered in the mire . . .

The Brontës in Winter

What is the secret of the constant appeal of Charlotte, Emily and Anne Brontë? Does it lie in the women themselves, in their books, or in Haworth on the moors in Yorkshire? Can it perhaps be found in that time of year around Christmas? Christmas figures a great deal in their

22

· A Yorkshire Christmas ·

*writing, not so much for its festivities, as for the
significant events in their own lives, many of which were
recorded by Elizabeth Gaskell in her biography of
Charlotte Brontë.*

Their mother and father, the curate of Hartshead in the parish of
Dewsbury, married on 29 December 1812. Five years later they
moved to the parish of Thornton near Bradford, and then on 25
February 1820 to Haworth, with their six children, Maria,
Elizabeth, Charlotte, Patrick (Branwell), Emily and Anne.

From their first going to Haworth, their walks were
directed rather out towards the heathery moors, sloping
upwards behind the parsonage, than towards the long
descending village street. A good old woman, who came to
nurse Mrs Brontë in the illness – an internal cancer – which
grew and gathered upon her, not many months after her arrival
at Haworth, tells that at that time the six little creatures used
to walk out, hand in hand, towards the glorious wild moors,
which in after days they loved so passionately; the elder ones
taking thoughtful care for the toddling wee things.

The girls were then sent to school at Cowan Bridge, a
cluster of some six or seven cottages gathered together at both
ends of a bridge over which the high road from Leeds to
Kendal crossed a little stream, called the Leck. Charlotte
confessed that this was the scene of Lowood in *Jane Eyre*, and
the school scenes were a repetition of Cowan Bridge.

Following the cold, damp winter of 1825, both Maria and
Elizabeth died. Charlotte and Emily left the school before the
following Christmas. Five years later, after Christmas,
Charlotte went to school at Roe Head, on the road from Leeds
to Huddersfield. One of the pupils recalls the first sight of
Charlotte, oddly dressed and odd-looking on that winter
morning, as 'sick for home she stood in tears' by the
school-room window, looking out on the snowy landscape.

It was about this time, at the age of fifteen, that she wrote the poem, 'The Wounded Stag'.

Passing amid the deepest shade
  Of the wood's sombre heart,
Last night I saw a wounded deer
  Laid lonely and apart.

Such light as pierced the crowded boughs
  (Light scattered, scant and dim,)
Passed through the fern that formed his couch
  And centred full on him.

Pain trembled in his weary limbs,
  Pain filled his patient eye,
Pain-crushed amid the shadowy fern
  His branchy crown did lie.

Where were his comrades? where his mate?
  All from his death-bed gone!
And he, thus struck and desolate,
  Suffered and bled alone.

Did he feel what a man might feel
  Friend-left, and sort distrest?
Did Pain's keen dart, and Grief's sharp sting
  Strive in his mangled breast?

Did longing for affection lost
  Barb every deadly dart;
Love unrepaid, and Faith betrayed
  Did these torment his heart?

No! leave to man his proper doom!
  These are the pangs that rise
Around the bed of state and gloom,
  Where Adam's offspring dies!

24

· A Yorkshire Christmas ·

Charlotte uses the imagery of Roe Head in her novel, *Shirley*, and once more uses December as the time of death of one of her characters, Captain Batt. Winter and Christmas she uses to great effect in *Jane Eyre* – her first meeting with Rochester in January on the moors, her self-inflicted pain at hearing of Rochester's Christmas party. In the Christmas holidays the Brontë sisters talked over their lives, and on Christmas Day 1836 declared their intention to write. They wrote to Robert Southey, the Poet Laureate, asking his opinion of their poems. The letter was dated 29 December. His reply was not exactly encouraging. 'Stringent' was how Charlotte described it.

The following Christmas, Charlotte had another weight on her mind.

I have said that Dewsbury Moor was low and damp, and that the air did not agree with her, though she herself was hardly aware how much her life there was affecting her health. But Anne had begun to suffer just before the holidays, and Charlotte watched over her younger sisters with the jealous vigilance of some wild creature, that changes her very nature if danger threatens her young. Anne had a slight cough, a pain at her side, a difficulty of breathing. Miss Wooler considered it as little more than a common cold; but Charlotte felt every indication of incipient consumption as a stab at her heart, remembering Maria and Elizabeth, whose places once knew them, and should know them no more.

But there was at least a happy Christmas in 1842:

Meanwhile, they enjoyed their Christmas all together inexpressibly. Branwell was with them; that was always a pleasure at this time; whatever might be his faults, or even

25

his vices, his sisters yet held him up as their family hope, as they trusted that he would some day be their family pride. They blinded themselves to the magnitude of the failings of which they were now and then told, by persuading themselves that such failings were common to all men of any strength of character, for, till sad experience taught them better, they fell into the usual error of confounding strong passions with strong character.

Charlotte's friend came over to see her, and she returned the visit. Her Brussels life must have seemed like a dream, so completely, in this short space of time, did she fall back into the old household ways; with more of household independence than she could ever have had during her aunt's life-time. Winter though it was, the sisters took their accustomed walks on the snow-covered moors; or went often down the long road to Keighley, for such books as had been added to the library there during their absence from England.

Emily, the mystical, silent sister, died six days before Christmas in 1848, followed three months later by the feckless, opium-poisoned brother, Branwell. Anne, the youngest sister, author of *The Tenant of Wildfell Hall*, died and was buried in Scarborough in 1849.

Charlotte was proposed to – at Christmas 1852 – by her father's curate, Arthur Bell Nicholls. One year later she was married – but not for long. 'On Christmas-day she and her husband walked to a poor old woman, carrying with them a great spice-cake to make glad her heart.'

As the winter ended at the end of March, Charlotte died.

The Battle of Wakefield – Christmas Eve 1460

EDWARD BAINES

Edward Baines (1744–1848) was a journalist and politician who became owner of the Leeds Mercury *in 1801 and Liberal MP for Leeds from 1834 to 1841. In 1823 he wrote the* History, Directory and Gazetteer of the County of York *from which this, and other extracts in this book, are taken.*

In the battle of Wakefield, fought on 24th December 1460, Richard Hanson, the brave Mayor of Hull, having greatly distinguished himself by his valour and intrepidity, fell covered with wounds, in the moment of victory, in the presence of his Queen.

No county in England has witnessed more of the civil wars to which Great Britain, in former ages, was exposed than Yorkshire, and Wakefield may rank amongst those towns in Yorkshire where this scourge of nations has prevailed in its utmost horrors.

The 'sore batell fought in the south feildes by the bridge', as mentioned by Leland, occupies a most distinguished place in English history. After the battle of Northampton, in which the Lancastrians sustained a signal defeat, and in which

Henry VI was taken prisoner, his Queen, Margaret of Anjou, repaired into the north, where she soon drew together an army of 20,000 men. The Duke of York, informed of her appearance in Yorkshire, hastened thither with a body of 5,000 men. Having arrived in the vicinity of Wakefield, he heard that the Queen was advancing towards him with greatly superior numbers. On this he resolved to retire to his castle at Sandal, and there to shut himself up till his eldest son, the Earl of Marche, who was levying troops on the borders of Wales, should arrive with the rest of his forces.

The Queen soon appeared before the walls of Sandal castle, with the main body of her army, led by the Dukes of Somerset and Exeter, provoking her enemy to battle, sometimes by menaces, and at other times by insults and defiances, observing that it was disgraceful for a man who aspired to a crown to suffer himself to be shut up by a woman.

This was more than he could endure. He quitted the castle and descended into the plain; and having drawn up his troops on Wakefield Green, he offered battle to the Lancastrians. The inequality of numbers was of itself sufficient to decide the victory, but the Queen having placed a body of troops in ambush under Lord Clifford and the Earl of Wiltshire, they fell upon the rear of the Duke's army, while they were attacked by the main body in front, and in less than half an hour the Duke himself was slain, and his little army was almost annihilated. His body was soon recognized amongst the slain, and his head cut off by Margaret's orders, and fixed upon the gates of York, with a paper crown upon it, in derision of his pretended title.

Clifford, whose thirst for blood seemed insatiable, plunged his murderous sword into the body of the Earl of Rutland, an interesting youth of seventeen, second son to the Duke of York, and 3,000 of his father's troops were on that day numbered amongst the dead.

It was the day before Christmas.

A Country Vet's Christmas

JAMES HERRIOT

James Herriot is the pseudonym of the most famous vet in the country, who settled into a North Yorkshire practice at Thirsk at the beginning of his career. Though now a successful author, he has never been tempted to leave the animals, the people and the countryside he knows so well. Even his national service in the RAF was spent at Scarborough! His books include All Creatures Great and Small, All Things Bright and Beautiful, All Things Wise and Wonderful *and* Let Sleeping Vets Lie, *from which this extract is taken.*

Inside the tiny living-room of the cottage I was ushered to the best chair by the fireside where two rough logs blazed and crackled.

'Bring cake out for Mr Herriot, mother,' the farmer cried as he rummaged in the pantry. He reappeared with a bottle of whisky at the same time as his wife bustled in carrying a cake thickly laid with icing and ornamented with coloured spangles, toboggans, reindeers.

Mr Kirby unscrewed the stopper. 'You know, mother, we're lucky to have such men as this to come out on a Christmas mornin' to help us.'

'Aye, we are that.' The old lady cut a thick slice of the cake and placed it on a plate by the side of an enormous wedge of Wensleydale cheese . . .

Pickering, 1947

Fletcher's butchers shop, Pickering, pre-1918

· A Yorkshire Christmas ·

I took a bite of the cake and followed it with a moist slice of cheese. When I had first come to Yorkshire I had been aghast when offered this unheard-of combination, but time had brought wisdom and I had discovered that the mixture when chewed boldly together was exquisite; and, strangely, I had also found that there was nothing more suitable for washing it finally over the tonsils than a draught of raw whisky.

'You don't mind t'wireless, Mr Herriot?' Mrs Kirby asked. 'We always like to have it on Christmas morning to hear t'old hymns but I'll turn it off if you like.'

'No, please leave it, it sounds grand.' I turned to look at the old radio with its chipped wooden veneer, the ornate scroll-work over the worn fabric; it must have been one of the earliest models and it gave off a tinny sound, but the singing of the church choir was none the less sweet. . . 'Hark the Herald Angels Sing' – flooding the little room, mingling with the splutter of the logs and the soft voices of the old people.

Rex Whistler's Wartime Christmas in Pickering

ALAN PICKUP

Alan Pickup, of Cuddy Brown Close, Pickering, attended the wartime Christmas party given for the children of the village by Rex Whistler and the Welsh Guards. He keeps a remarkable collection of old photographs, some of which are included in this book.

It was the Christmas of 1943 that the 2nd Battalion of Welsh Guards were stationed at Pickering and Rex Whistler, who was an officer with them, was not lucky enough to get leave. So to help pass the time he made the suggestion that the regiment should provide a Christmas tea and entertainment for 250 local children between the ages of six and nine in the Memorial Hall on 24th December. Rex Whistler described what happened in a letter to his mother:

> Our Christmas Party here was a big success I gather, and we 'clocked in' 294 children, not counting a fair sprinkling of others who came in with their mothers — children of the Regiment, etc., too young to come alone. So we had well over 300 to tea in all. The hall certainly did look very gay.

Rex Whistler

There is a big stage at one end, on either side of which I painted an enormous Guardsman (10 or 11 ft high) in full dress, bearskin and all, then on the stage curtain which was kept lowered, we contrived a vast Regimental device with glittering crown and huge leek in green shining tinsel etc., etc. There were great festoons of evergreens and the whole ceiling a dizzy mass of flags and bunting. The tables were arranged like an E but with four arms instead of three and all lit with candles and covered with crackers! (which we were lucky to find). At one side there was a huge Christmas Tree blazing with lights, and on another the Battalion dance band bellowed away with carols and popular songs – to all of which the children sang at the tops of their voices – which was charming, wasn't it? and it made the party 'go'.

During tea, to deafening shrieks of excitement, Father C was seen descending a high stairway from the room above in a cloud of falling snow. After tea a Punch and Judy arrived and that was followed by a conjuror, then a general mêlée, and after God Save the King, hat and coat finding for about an hour! But there were no casualties and no one was spotted blubbing. A miracle surely!

It was typical of his nature that he should devote so much of his time to bringing such joy and pleasure to so many children during wartime conditions on the last Christmas Eve he would know, as a few months later his regiment were to go over to France for the Normandy landings in which he was to lose his life.

I can still recall peeping into the Memorial Hall on that Saturday morning and seeing Whistler up a ladder busily putting the finishing touches to his pair of guardsmen. It was a great shame that his murals, instead of being painted on canvas, were done directly on to the walls, because twenty-five years later the old stone walls were to peel and crumble and

Rex Whistler's Christmas Mural

there was no way in which his handiwork could in the circumstances be retained.

One link with this era of Rex Whistler and his stay in Pickering, apart from memories of this event, is a copy of the photograph of Whistler in battle dress tunic.

Rex Whistler, 1905 to 1944, was also noted for fanciful murals which decorated the Tate Gallery Restaurant, Haddon Hall, Pickering Memorial Hall and the bathroom of the house in Beacon Park, Pickering, where he lodged whilst stationed at Castle Camp in Pickering.

The Terrible Knitters of the Dales

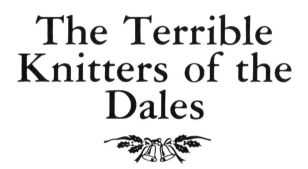

William Howitt, in The Rural Life of England *(1844), describes the knitting parties which were prevalent in the Dales, especially during the dark winter days around Christmas; and Robert Southey, in* The Doctor, *records the actual words of 'The Terrible Knitters of Dent'.*

Knitting Parties

Men, women, and children, all knit. Formerly you might have met the waggoners knitting as they went along with their teams; but this is now rare; for the greater influx of visitors, and their wonder expressed at this and other practices, have made them rather ashamed of them, and shy of strangers observing them. But the men still knit a great deal in the houses; and the women knit incessantly. They have knitting schools, where the children are taught; and where they sing in chorus knitting songs, some of which appear as childish as the nursery songs of the last generation. Yet all of them bear some reference to their employment and mode of life; and the chorus, which maintains regularity of action and keeps up the attention, is of more importance than the words. Here is a specimen:

36

The Terrible Knitters

Bell-wether o' Barking, cries baa, baa,
How many sheep have we lost today?
Nineteen we have lost, one have we faun'
Run Rockie, run Rockie, run, run, run.

[Barking is the name of a mountain near Dent, Rockie was the name of a shepherd's dog.]

This is sung while they knit one round of the stocking; when the second round commences they begin again:

Bell-wether o' Barking, cries baa, baa,
How many sheep have we lost today?
Eighteen we have lost, two have we faun'
Run Rockie, run Rockie, run, run, run.

and so on till they have knit twenty rounds, decreasing the numbers on the one hand, and increasing them on the other.

These songs are sung not only by the children in the schools, but also by the people at their sittings, which are social assemblies of the neighbourhood, not for eating and drinking, but merely for society. As soon as it becomes dark, and the usual business of the day is over, and the young children are put to bed, they rake or put out the fire; take their cloaks and lanterns, and set out with their knitting to the house of the neighbour, where the sitting falls in rotation, for it is a regularly circulating assembly from house to house through the particular neighbourhood. The whole troop of neighbours being collected, they sit and knit, singing knitting songs, and tell knitting-stories. Here all the old stories and traditions of the dale come up, and they often get so excited that they say 'Neighbours, we'll not part tonight,' that is, till after twelve o'clock. All this time their knitting goes on with unremitting speed. They sit, rocking to and fro like so many weird wizards. They burn no candle, but knit by the light of the peat fire. And this rocking motion is connected with a mode of knitting peculiar to the place, called swaving, which is difficult to describe. Ordinary knitting is performed by a variety of little motions, but this is a single uniform tossing motion of both hands at once, and the body accompanying it with a sort of sympathetic action.

The neighbouring dale, Garsdale, which is a narrower and more secluded one than Dent, is a great knitting dale. The old men sit there in companies around the fire, and so intent are they on their occupation and stories, that they pin cloths on their shins to prevent them being burnt; and sometimes they may be seen on a bench at the house-front, and whence they have come out to cool themselves, sitting in a row knitting with their shin-cloths on, making the oddest appearance imaginable.

The Terrible Knitters of Dent

> Sally an' I, Sally an' I,
> For a good pudding pye,
> Taa hoaf wheat, an' tudder hoaf rye,
> Sally an' I, for a good pudding pye.

We sang this (altering t'neams) at every needle: and when we com at t'end cried 'off' an' began again, an' sea we strave on o' t'day through.

We were stawed, as I telt yea – o' t'pleser we hed was when we went out a bit to beat t'fire for a nebbor 'at was baking – that was a grand day for us! – At Kursmas [Christmas] teea, ther was t'Maskers – an' on Kursmas day at mworn they gav us sum reed stuff to t'Breakfast – I think it maun ha' been Jocklat – but we dud'nt like 't at a', 't ommost puzzened us – an' we cared for nought but how we were to git back to Langdon – Neet an' Day there was nought but this knitting. T'nebbors ust at gang about fra' house to house, we' ther wark, – than yan fire dud, ye knaw, an' they cud hev a better – they hed girt lang black peeats – an' set them up an hed in a girt round we' a whole at top – an a't'Fwoak sat about it. When ony o' them gat into a hubble we' ther wark, they shouted out 'turn a Peeat' – an' them 'at sat nearest t'fire turnt yan, an' meaad a low – for they nivver hed onny cannal. – We knat quorse wosset stockings – some gloves – an' some neet caps, an' wastecwoat breests, an' petticwoats. I yance knat a stocking, for mysell, e' six hours – Sally yan e'sebben – an' t'woman's Doughter, 'at was aulder than us e'eight – an' they sent a nwote to our Fwoak e'Langdon at tell them.

Sally an' me, when we wer by our sells, wer always contrivin' how we were at git away, when we sleept by oursells we talk't of nought else – but when t'woman's Doughter sleept we' us we were qwhite mum – summat or udder always

happent at hinder us, till yan day, between Kursmas an' Cannalmas, when t'woman's Doughter stait at heaam, we teuk off.

Afore we gat to Sebber we fell hungry; an' ther was a fine, girt, reed house nut far off t'rwoad, whar we went an' begged for a bit o' breead – but they wadd'nt give us ought – sea we trampt on, an come to a lile theakt house, an' I said – 'Sally, thou shall beg t'neesht – thou's less than me, an' mappen they'll sarra us' – an' they dud – an' gav us a girt shive of bread – at last we gat to Scotch Jins, as they ca't'public House about three mile fra Sebber (o' this side) – a Scotch woman kept it. – It was amaist dark, sea we axt her at let us stay o'neet – she teuk us in, an' gave us sum boilt milk and breead – an' suun put us to bed – we telt her our taael; an' she sed we wer int' reet at run away . . .

It was twea o'clock int'mworning when we gat to our awn Duir – I ca'ed out 'Fadder. Fadder. – Mudder. Mudder.' ower an' ower again – She hard us, an' sed – 'That's our Betty's voice' – 'Thus's nought but fancies, lig still,' said my Fadder – but she waddent; and sea gat up, an' opent' Duir and there warr we stanning doddering – and daized we'cauld, as neer deead as macks nea matter – When she so us she was mare flate than we – She brast out a crying – an' we grat – an' my Fadder grat an'a' – an' they duddent flight, nor said nought tull us, for cumming away, – they warrant a bit angert – an' my Fadder sed we sud nivver gang back again.

Lewis Carroll's Christmas Magazines

The real name of the creator of *Alice in Wonderland* was Charles Lutwidge Dodgson. Twenty-five years of his early life were spent in the North Riding, at Croft by the Tees.

On Sundays, 'Lewis Carroll' went with his family to the quaint old St Peter's Church at Croft to hear his father, the Rector, preach. The Clervaux, Milbankes and Chaytors had all worshipped and were buried there. Byron had brought his unhappy bride from Halnaby Hall to sit in the red-curtained Milbanke pew, and George Hudson, the Railway King, had shown his boredom by turning his back to the parson, while his wife put up her parasol during the sermon.

Charles, aided by the village carpenter, made a troupe of marionettes and a puppet theatre. He wrote all the plays himself. One of the most popular was 'La Guida di Bragia', a ballad opera in which he poked fun at Bradshaw's Railway Guide. His sisters would show their appreciation of his 'funny' plays by shrieking with laughter at his witty lines. He also entertained them by dressing in a long white cloak and wearing a brown wig to perform conjuring shows, in the nursery or for Christmas parties.

In the dark winter days around Christmas, he would produce family magazines containing his own poems, stories and sketches. The first magazine, 'Useful and Instructive

41

· *A Yorkshire Christmas* ·

Poetry', was full of nonsense verse, which he later developed in
Alice in Wonderland, published at Christmas, 1870.

> He thought he saw a Buffalo
>   Upon the chimney-piece:
> He looked again, and found it was
>   His sister's husband's niece.
> 'Unless you leave this house', he said,
>   'I'll send for the Police!'
>
> He thought he saw a Rattlesnake
>   That questioned him in Greek,
> He looked again and found it was
>   The Middle of Next Week.
> 'The one thing I regret,' he said,
>   'Is that it cannot speak!'
>
> He thought he saw a Banker's Clerk
>   Descending from the bus:
> He looked again, and found it was
>   A Hippopotamus:
> 'If this should stay to dine,' he said,
>   'There won't be much for us.'

'What is the use of a book,' thought Alice, 'without
pictures or conversations?'

When he was twelve years old, Charles went to Richmond
Grammar School. He stayed at the school for only eighteen
months, and when he left at Christmas, 1845, his final report
by the headmaster said:

Be assured that I shall always feel a peculiar interest in the
gentle, and well conducted boy who is now leaving us.

His father, by this time, had been made chaplain to the Bishop of Ripon, then Canon of Ripon Cathedral, and Archdeacon of Richmond.

At Christmas in 1854, Charles graduated at Christ Church College, Oxford, and he returned to spend his Christmas holiday in Croft and Ripon. At Croft, he produced a scrap-book magazine called 'Mischmasch', which contained the four most original lines of English poetry – his first piece of Anglo-Saxon nonsense which had its origins in Yorkshire and across the border in neighbouring Durham, where Sir John Conyers slew the Sockburn Dragon. The itch to baffle, mystify and entertain into the bargain remained with him till his death.

Jabberwocky

'Twas brillig and the slithy toves
Did gyre and gimble in the wabe:
All mimsy were the borogoves,
And the mome raths outgrabe.

Alice's opinion of the poem is: 'It's very pretty, but *rather* hard to understand', but Humpty Dumpty translates the difficult words thus: '*Brillig* means four o'clock in the afternoon – *slithy* means lithe and slimy. *Toves* are something like badgers, and lizards – and corkscrews too. To *gyre* is to go round and round like a gyroscope, and to *gimble* is to make holes like a gimlet. A *wabe* is a grass plot around a sun-dial, and *mimsy* is flimsy and miserable. A *borogove* is a thin shabby-looking bird, *mome* is short for home, *raths* are sorts of green pigs, and *outgrabing* is something between bellowing and whistling.'

Carroll is known to have modelled his White Knight upon himself. Both had shaggy hair, a gentle face, mild blue eyes, and a topsy-turvy outlook on the world. What's more, they had a mutual fondness for tricks and gadgets. Carroll, like his much-practised character, was not just a 'great hand at

inventing things'. He took delight in showing off the results to a captive audience. Like the White Knight with his 'queer-shaped little deal box', he always travelled with a black bag of secrets, into which he would dip to produce mysteries on train journeys or at the seaside. Carroll himself invented the prototype of the miniature travelling chess set, with holes to prevent the pegged men from falling over, and the first double-sided adhesive tape: '1896 – Invented a substitute for gum, for fastening envelopes (as used to be done with wafers), mounting small things in books, etc. – viz: paper with gum on *both* sides. It should be supplied in sheets, and also in discs.' He also invented a game which one may assume to have evolved into 'Scrabble'. 'December 19, 1880 – The idea occurred to me that a game might be made of letters, to be moved about on a chess-board till they form words.'

For Lewis Carroll, the greatest joy in life was being with children. 'Three-quarters of my life are children' he said – 'the deepest and purest pleasure in this world.' Apart from his own family, he seldom made adult friends. His relations with them were hampered by his stammer, part-deafness and a natural sensitivity which made normal social contact difficult. With children it was different – especially little girls. They loved him and seemed to understand him, seeing through the shyness to the fun-loving boy that lay hidden beneath his protective mask. 'I am fond of all children (except boys)!' he said.

> I'll tell thee everything I can:
>   There's little to relate.
> I saw an aged, aged man,
>   A-sitting on a gate.
>
> He said, 'I look for butterflies
>   That sleep among the wheat:
> I make them into mutton-pies,
>   And sell them in the street.'

44

A letter to a young friend, Christmas 1873

My Dear Gaynor,

As to dancing, my dear, I *never* dance, unless I am allowed to do it in my own peculiar way. The last house I tried it in, the floor broke through. But then it was a poor sort of floor – the beams were only six inches thick, hardly worth calling beams at all; stone arches are much more sensible when any dancing *of my peculiar* kind, is to be done.

At New Year in 1898 Carroll became seriously ill, and as he lay dying he said to his sisters, 'Take away these pillows. I shall not need them again.'

> Without, the frost, the blinding snow,
>   The storm-wind's moody madness –
> Within, the firelight ruddy glow,
>   And childhood's nest of gladness.
> The magic words shall hold thee fast:
>   Thou shalt not heed the raving blast.

The Life of Charlotte Brontë

ELIZABETH GASKELL

When Charlotte Brontë died in 1855 her father, the Revd Patrick Brontë, asked Mrs Gaskell to write a life of his daughter as a fitting and imperishable memorial to her genius.

Men hardly past middle life talk of the days of their youth, spent in this part of the country, when, during the winter months, they rode up to the saddle-girths in mud; when absolute business was the only reason for stirring beyond the precincts of home; and when that business was conducted under a pressure of difficulties which they themselves, borne along to Bradford market in a swift first-class carriage, can hardly believe to have been possible. For instance, one woollen manufacturer says that, not five-and-twenty years ago, he had to rise betimes to set off on a winter's morning in order to be at Bradford with the great waggon-load of goods manufactured by his father: this load was packed over-night, but in the morning there was great gathering around it, and flashing of lanterns, and examination of horses' feet, before the ponderous waggon got under weigh; and then some one had to go groping here and there, on hands and knees, and always sounding with a staff down the long, steep, slippery brow, to find where the horses might tread safely, until they reached the

comparative easy-going of the deep-rutted main road. People went on horseback over the upland moors, following the tracks of the packhorses that carried the parcels, baggage, or goods from one town to another, between which there did not happen to be a highway.

But in the winter, all such communication was impossible, by reason of the snow which lay long and late on the bleak high ground. I have known people who, travelling by the mail-coach over Blackstone Edge, had been snowed up for a week or ten days, at the little inn near the summit, and obliged to spend both Christmas and New Year's Day there, till the store of provisions laid in for the use of the landlord and his family falling short before the inroads of the unexpected visitors, they had recourse to the turkeys, geese, and Yorkshire pies with which the coach was laden; and even these were beginning to fail, when a fortunate thaw released them from their prison.

Christmas 1849

The winter of this year in the north was hard and cold; it affected Miss Brontë's health less than usual, however, probably because the change and the medical advice she had taken in London had done her good; probably, also, because her friend had come to pay her a visit, and enforced that attention to bodily symptoms which Miss Brontë was too apt to neglect, from a fear of becoming nervous herself about her own state, and thus infecting her father. But she could scarcely help feeling much depressed in spirits as the anniversary of her sister Emily's death came round [19 December]; all the recollections connected with it were painful, yet there were no outward events to call off her attention, and prevent them from pressing hard upon her. At this time, as at many others, I find her alluding in her letters to the solace which she found in the books sent her from Cornhill.

· A Yorkshire Christmas ·

What, I sometimes ask, could I do without them? I have recourse to them as to friends; they shorten and cheer many an hour that would be too long and too desolate otherwise; even when my tired sight will not permit me to continue reading, it is pleasant to see them on the shelf, or on the table. I am still very rich, for my stock is far from exhausted. Some other friends have sent me books lately. The perusal of Harriet Martineau's *Eastern Life* has afforded me great pleasure; and I have found a deep and interesting subject of study in Newman's work on the *Soul*. Have you read this work? It is daring, – it may be mistaken, – but it is pure and elevated. Froude's *Nemesis of Faith* I did not like; I thought it morbid; yet in its pages, too, are found sprinklings of truth.

By this time, 'Airedale, Wharfedale, Calderdale, and Ribblesdale' all knew the place of residence of 'Currer Bell' [Charlotte Brontë's pseudonym]. She compared herself to the ostrich hiding its head in the sand; and says that she still buries hers in the heath of Haworth moors; but 'the concealment is but self-delusion'.

Indeed it was. Far and wide in the West Riding had spread the intelligence that Currer Bell was no other than a daughter of the venerable clergyman of Haworth; the village itself caught up the excitement.

Mr ——, having finished *Jane Eyre*, is now crying out for the 'other book;' he is to have it next week . . . Mr R—— has finished *Shirley*; he is delighted with it. John ——'s wife seriously thought him gone wrong in the head, as she heard him giving vent to roars of laughter as he sat alone, clapping and stamping on the floor. He would read all the scenes about the curates aloud to papa.

Martha came in yesterday, puffing and blowing, and

48

much excited. 'I've heard sich news!' she began. 'What about?' 'Please, ma'am, you've been and written two books – the grandest books that ever was seen. My father has heard it at Halifax, and Mr G—— T—— and Mr G—— and Mr M—— at Bradford; and they are going to have a meeting at the Mechanics' Institute, and to settle about ordering them.' 'Hold your tongue, Martha, and be off.' I fell into a cold sweat. *Jane Eyre* will be read by J—— B——, by Mrs T——, and B——. Heaven help, keep, and deliver me!

The Haworth people have been making great fools of themselves about *Shirley*; they have taken it in an enthusiastic light. When they got the volumes at the Mechanics' Institute, all the members wanted them. They cast lots for the whole three, and whoever got a volume was only allowed to keep it two days, and was to be fined a shilling per diem for longer detention. It would be mere nonsense and vanity to tell you what they say.

The tone of these extracts is thoroughly consonant with the spirit of Yorkshire and Lancashire people, who try as long as they can to conceal their emotions of pleasure under a bantering exterior, almost as if making fun of themselves. Miss Brontë was extremely touched in the secret places of her warm heart by the way in which those who had known her from childhood were proud and glad of her success. All round about the news had spread; strangers came 'from beyond Burnley' to see her, as she went quietly and unconsciously into church; and the sexton 'gained many a half-crown' for pointing her out.

Tricki's Christmas Hamper

JAMES HERRIOT

A second extract from the Yorkshire vet's books, this time from If Only They Could Talk.

Driving home, I mused on the many advantages of being Tricki's uncle. When he went to the seaside he sent me boxes of oak-smoked kippers; and when the tomatoes ripened in his greenhouse, he sent a pound or two every week. Tins of tobacco arrived regularly, sometimes with a photograph carrying a loving inscription.

But it was when the Christmas hamper arrived from Fortnum and Mason's that I decided that I was on a really good thing which should be helped along a bit. Hitherto, I had merely rung up and thanked Mrs Pumphrey for the gifts, and she had been rather cool, pointing out that it was Tricki who had sent the things and he was the one who should be thanked.

With the arrival of the hamper it came to me, blindingly, that I had been guilty of a grave error of tactics. I set myself to compose a letter to Tricki. Avoiding Siegfried's sardonic eye, I thanked my doggy nephew for his Christmas gifts and for all his generosity in the past. I expressed my sincere hopes that the festive fare had not upset his delicate digestion and suggested that if he did experience any discomfort he should have recourse to the black powder his uncle always prescribed. A vague feeling of professional shame was easily swamped by

floating visions of kippers, tomatoes and hampers. I addressed the envelope to Master Tricki Pumphrey, Barlby Grange and slipped it into the post box with only a slight feeling of guilt.

On my next visit, Mrs Pumphrey drew me to one side. 'Mr Herriot,' she whispered. 'Tricki adored your charming letter and he will keep it always, but he was very put out about one thing – you addressed it to Master Tricki and he does insist upon Mister. He was dreadfully affronted at first, quite beside himself, but when he saw it was from you he soon recovered his good temper. I can't think why he should have these little prejudices. Perhaps it is because he is an only dog – I do think an only dog develops more prejudices than one from a large family.'

Christmas Disaster on the Settle to Carlisle Line

Any mention of railways and the Dales almost certainly invokes references to the Leeds–Settle–Carlisle line – over 100 miles of bleak moorland scenery where the railway has become a welcome feature of the rugged fells.

Much of the line between Garsdale and Dent is protected by windbreaks and snow barriers, but these have

not prevented engines being buried to the tops of their funnels, and whole trains, track and station buildings, being completely lost for days and weeks.

Built by the Midland Railway purely to score points over its rivals, it has been dubbed 'the line that no one wanted'. More significantly, it is a superb monument to all things Victorian. The twenty-four tall arches of the Ribblehead viaduct are now an essential element of the landscape, and a great engineering achievement.

If Ribblehead is its masterpiece, it may prove to be the greatest stumbling block to the future of the line, as its crumbling masonry, ravaged by wind, rain and frost, cries out for cash to be spent on its maintenance. So strong is the wind across the moors that not a few trains have lost their freight, blown off the viaduct, and many a railwayman has lost his train altogether in the snow.

A handful of people still remember the disaster near Hawes Junction/Garsdale which occurred in the early hours of Christmas Eve, 1910. Traffic had been heavy on the line through the evening, with main-line as well as local trains, due to Christmas. Otherwise it was a normal night at Hawes for Signalman Sutton. A wild wind blew and rain was falling; wintry showers swirled off the fells and beat on the windows of the signal box.

Two fast goods trains passed through on the up line. After a time the signals were cleared for the main line, but two engines for Carlisle which had been waiting at Hawes set off, believing they had been cleared. A third engine was just completing its circuit on the turntable at Hawes, intending to join the other two, but the signal was against it. Driver George Tempest stood waiting and wondering.

Then he heard the low rumble of a fast train on the up line and saw the St Pancras to Glasgow midnight sleeper express

· A Yorkshire Christmas ·

Ribblehead Viaduct

Dent Station, 1947

thunder past. He turned to his fireman. There was a long, thin blast of an engine whistle — a dull thump — and then silence.

'He's catched 'em,' said Tempest.

The express had piled into both trains ahead, derailing all three. Then the high pressure gas main which lit the express ruptured and exploded. A shepherd on the fells saw the whole train engulfed in a single brilliant flash of flame. The alarm was raised, but twelve passengers perished.

Signalman Sutton said later that he then realised with horror that he had forgotten about the Carlisle engines when he had cleared the signals. To his relief signalman he said, 'Will you go to Stationmaster Bunce and say that I'm afraid I have wrecked the Scotch express!'

The First Festival of Christmas at York

EDWARD BAINES

Among the most celebrated of the British monarchs before the Norman Conquest was King Arthur. This monarch expelled the Saxons from York, and almost from the Island, in the year 520, by the sanguinary battle of Baden Hills, in which 90,000 of the enemy were slain. Arthur, after the defeat of the Saxons, undertook an expedition into Scotland, with a determination

to destroy that ancient seat of enmity from one end to the other.

From this purpose he was dissuaded by the Bishops. The Scots had just received the gospel, and it was represented to the King, by his spiritual guides, in the true spirit of that religion which he professed, that Christians ought not to spill the blood of Christians – a maxim, that has unfortunately for the world, not been sufficiently inculcated in modern times.

Arthur, after his expedition to Scotland, returned to York, where he convened an assembly of the clergy and people, to heal the divisions, and to regulate the affairs of the church.

At this time, this great monarch, and his clergy, with the nobility, and the soldiers, kept their Christmas, in York. This was the first festival of the kind ever celebrated in Britain, and from which, all those ever since held have taken their model. 'The latter end of December,' says the historian [Buchanan], 'was spent in mirth, jollity, drinking, and the vices that are too often their consequences, so that the representations of the old heathenish feasts, dedicated to Saturn, were here again revived. Gifts were sent mutually from one to another,

frequent invitations passed between friends, and domestic offenders were not punished. All this, was to celebrate the nativity of Christ, then, as they say, born.'

Arthur, after all his glory, had the misfortune to be slain in a rebellion of his own subjects, and by the hands of his own nephew.

'On the Post' at Christmas

RICHARD METCALFE

Richard Metcalfe, a Yorkshireman, is a senior officer of the University of Durham and a Tutor of Hatfield College.

Twenty years ago the Post Office at Christmas time relied on vast numbers of 'casuals' to help cope with the great increase in traffic, and for six years I was one of a small army of sixth-formers and students who spent the ten days or so leading up to Christmas 'on the post', in my case at Barnsley Head Post Office.

When we signed on we were given an armband with a duty number on and a buff card, listing duties and containing an extract from the Official Secrets Act, which we had to sign. As

I walked the streets or sorted mail I used to wonder what possible use it would be to the Russians to know how a letter posted in Cudworth reached its destination in Wombwell. The armband was much more useful – it meant we travelled free on the buses while on duty.

For my first year I was assigned to the parcels section, which for the Christmas period set up camp in the Territorial Army Drill Hall on Eastgate. From there, as frequently as we could manage, two of us were despatched around the town centre propelling a large wicker basket, lettered 'G.P.O.', mounted on cartwheels. Using this relic of the past we delivered all manner of parcels to shops and offices; most were of little interest, but we did have turkeys with their feet sticking out of muslin sacks, and packages of not-terribly-fresh salmon from Scotland.

This first year did not prove to be a great personal economic success. I desperately wanted a donkey-jacket, to be like all my friends at school, and I persuaded my mother to lend me £3 17s. 6d. to buy one on the grounds that I needed it for working out of doors. Then disaster struck – the parcels stopped arriving in such great numbers and we were paid off. My total wage was £3 7s. 6d. I was ten shillings out of pocket and, to add insult to injury, had to borrow more money to buy my parents their Christmas present.

The next four Christmas periods I spent on the 'walks', and quickly found what a fascinating insight could be gained into people's lives from the post they received. At one end of the spectrum were people who watched anxiously as you worked your way along the street, waiting for the registered packet containing social security payments; then there was the upwardly mobile family who had gone to Benidorm for Christmas and sent a postcard to every single house in the street, just to make sure that everyone knew; and there was the old man in a bungalow who watched for me every day and waved hopefully, but never received a single letter.

This was the year the Government decided to extend British Summer Time into the winter. Whatever the intended effect, in Barnsley it meant that for many people about half the working day was spent in the dark. The Post Office issued us with cycle-lamps which clipped on to our jacket lapels, carefully designed so that the beam would shine neither into the pouch nor on to house numbers, nor anywhere else of any use.

It was on one of these dark mornings that I knocked on a door in Worsbrough Dale to collect the 8d. owing in the

absence of any stamp on the envelope. There was no reply, but as I was walking away a head appeared in a bedroom window. The door was eventually opened by a pyjama-clad man. He apologised because he was on nights, and I apologised for waking him up. Amid this festive civility, he rummaged around for the 8d. and I turned away, only to be recalled again to see his civility evaporate as he shouted, 'Hey up, young 'un – tha's got mi aht o' mi bed and takken eightpence off mi for a card . . . from mi bloody mother-in-law!'

It was in the next street the following Saturday that I received the hallmark of all real postmen – that is, I was bitten by a dog. My success in coping with various alsatians and labradors lulled me into a sense of false security when confronted by a Yorkshire terrier, which leapt up and bit me behind the knee. Back at the delivery office I was welcomed like a war hero, made to fill in the inevitable form, and despatched to Beckett Hospital. In best casualty department tradition, about 50 of us were kept waiting for three hours, the sole diversion being to watch the needles drop off the Christmas tree, until a doctor appeared and tried to deal with everyone at once. The first thing he asked was why I had a torch on my lapel in the middle of the day. My reply that 'it was dark when I arrived at the hospital' did little to foster relationships, and he curtly told the sister to give me a tetanus jab in my backside. The sister pointed out that I would have to wait ages for a cubicle and suggested that, if my modesty would permit, it would save everyone a lot of time if I would expose the relevant part of my body there in the waiting room. And so it was that I had my first tetanus booster jab in a room full of people, separated from their gaze only by the fortunately ample figure of the sister.

For my final spell at the Post Office I was made time-keeper. This meant that I spent the whole day in the warmth of the delivery office, despatching fellow students on their walks.

This turned out to be less straightforward than it seemed, since in those days before sexual equality, while a man could carry up to 40 lbs in his pouch, a woman was restricted to 30 lbs, and some of the smaller girls were struggling with that.

There were also problems when some students brought back more letters than they had delivered, claiming that whole streets had disappeared without trace. By far the worst case was a geography student (I regret to say, from my own University) who brought back from his first round the entire contents of his pouch. For his second attempt he was armed with a street map and copious instructions, but still returned with a pouch two-thirds full. Finally we switched him to a walk which consisted of about half a mile along one main road, the most complicated requirement being to cross the road when Barnsley ended and come back down the other side. When he returned with a half-full pouch, there was no alternative but to send him for the early bath!

I enjoyed these experiences so much that I was moved to apply to the Post Office as a trainee manager. Unfortunately my intimate knowledge of postal deliveries in Barnsley seemed to count for little at the final interview board in London, and I was rejected. The letter telling me this ironically went to the wrong address, and I consoled myself by thinking that it was perhaps better if the Post Office and I parted company while my memories were confined to those six Christmas times in Barnsley.

1967 Christmas Stamps

St Michael-le-Belfry in York was the church, and the painting in the reredos was the subject, chosen by the GPO for the threepenny stamp in its Christmas issue of 1967. *The Adoration of the Shepherds*, seen all over the world, was copied from a Spanish painting and dedicated on Michaelmas Eve 1926 by the Archdeacon of York.

The Scaffold at Christmas

EDWARD BAINES

The treachery of Sir John Hotham, the governor of the town of Hull, which had already begun to be suspected by parliament, induced them to watch his movements and the appointment of Lord Fairfax to the office of general of the army of the North,

gave deadly umbrage to the baronet, who aspired to that honour, and induced him to seek opportunities to deliver up Hull to the royalists. Into this conspiracy, his son, Captain Hotham, very readily entered, and became the medium of negotiation for the accomplishment of this treacherous purpose.

The Mayor of Hull, Thos. Raikes, Esq. having learnt, that the plot for delivering up the town was now ripe for execution, held a consultation with the chiefs of the parliamentary party, and it was resolved to defeat the project by seizing the governor and his son.

On the 29th of June, 1643, Captain Moyer, who commanded the ship Hercules, stationed by parliament in the Humber, landed a hundred men from his ship, and seized the Castle and block houses almost without resistance. About the same time, 1500 of the soldiers and inhabitants, who had been waiting in the town for the word of command from the mayor, seized the main-guard, near the magazine, and next took possession of all the artillery on the walls. These measures having so far succeeded, Captain Hotham was then secured, and a guard was placed at the door of the governor's house; all this was effected in the space of about an hour, and without the shedding of a drop of blood.

Sir John Hotham having in the mean time obtained information of what was transacting, found means to escape, but being secured by Captain Boynton, in Beverley, the governor was conveyed under a strong guard to Hull, where he was put on board the Hercules, together with his son, Captain Hotham, and conveyed to London.

The catastrophe is universally known: after a long and strict confinement, Sir John Hotham was brought before a court-martial, at Guildhall, in London, on the 30th of November, charged with 'traitorously betraying the trust reposed in him by parliament,' which charge being clearly substantiated, the

court, on the 7th of December, pronounced sentence, that he should suffer death, by having his head severed from his body.

Two days after the conviction of his father, Captain Hotham was arraigned before the court martial, charged with 'having betrayed the trust reposed in him by the parliament, and with perfidiously adhering to the enemy.' This charge was supported by satisfactory evidence, and the son was condemned to die in the same way as his father.

On the 1st of January, Captain Hotham was brought to the scaffold, on Tower-hill, and underwent the sentence of the law; and on the day following, Sir John suffered decapitation, upon the scaffold at the same place – the victim of his own inconstancy and want of resolution.

The fate of Sir John Hotham and of his son, called to the mind of the king, the imprecation of – 'May God bring confusion on me and mine, if I be not a faithful and loyal subject to your majesty!' This profane denunciation, it will be remembered, was uttered at the time when Sir John refused to admit the king into Hull, and Charles considered the execution of the governor as a visitation of Providence for his disloyalty, for which his subsequent repentance was not sufficient to atone; but this case, considered in connexion with Charles's own fate, may serve to show the danger of writing the judgments of heaven upon the sufferings of our adversaries, for the question naturally arises, if the execution of Sir John Hotham, by parliament, in 1644, was a judgment of heaven, what name must be given to the execution of the king, in 1648, under the sanction of the same authority?

Christmas Greetings – From a Fairy to a Child

LEWIS CARROLL

LADY dear, if fairies may
   For a moment lay aside
Cunning tricks and elfish play,
   'Tis at happy Christmas-tide.

We have heard the children say –
   Gentle children, whom we love –
Long ago on Christmas-Day,
   Came a message from above.

Still, as Christmas-tide comes round,
   They remember it again –
Echo still the joyful sound
   'Peace on earth, good-will to men!'

Yet the hearts must child-like be
   Where such heavenly guests abide,
Unto children, in their glee,
   All the year is Christmas-tide.

Thus, forgetting tricks and play
For a moment, Lady dear,
We would wish you, if we may,
Merry Christmas, glad New Year!

Christmas 1867

from

South Riding

WINIFRED HOLTBY

Winifred Holtby (1893–1935), born at Rudston, Yorkshire, was a journalist, critic, feminist, pacifist and author of six novels, South Riding *being winner of the James Tait Black Memorial Prize.*

Life at Willow Lodge moved through a cycle of festivities – Christmas, Easter, Whitsun and the Summer Holidays – with smaller feast-days interspersed between them, horse-shows, bazaars, the Flintonbridge Point-to-Point, the High School Speech Days.

But of all these focal points the most active, persistent and inescapable was Christmas. The season began almost as soon as

65

the little boys ran round the Kiplington streets shouting 'Penny for the Old Guy' on frosty November evenings; long before notices went up in the lighted Kingsport windows, 'Please Shop Early,' its imminence overshadowed all other Beddows' activities; it rose slowly to its climax with the carving of the family turkey at midday dinner on Christmas Day, and subsided gradually through Boxing Day, the maids' holidays, indigestion and crumbling evergreen decorations until the old calendars could be thrown away, the garlands taken down, and the New Year had come.

All through the year Mrs Beddows and her family set themselves to accumulate the objects which she could bestow as gifts at Christmas. In a chest on the front landing known as the glory hole they stored the harvest of bazaars and birthdays, of raffles, bridge-drive prizes, bargain sales, and even presents which they had themselves received at former Christmases. Into the glory hole went blotters, pen-wipers, and painted vases, dessert d'oylies, table-centres and imitation fruits of wax or velvet, lampshades, knitted bed-jackets and embroidered covers for the *Radio Times*, all the bric-à-brac of civil exchange or time-killing occupation. The indictment of a social system lay in those drawers if they but knew it – a system which over-works eight-tenths of its female population, and gives the remaining two-tenths so little to do that they must clutter the world with useless objects. Mrs Beddows did not see it quite like that; presents were presents; bazaars were bazaars, and Sybil was teaching the Women's Institute class raffia work and glove-making. Surely these were good things? She did not question further.

Early in the month the contents of the glory hole were brought down into the dining-room and sorted. Aunt Ursula's plant pot might do for the Rectory people; but Mr Peckover's framed verse 'A Garden is a lovesame thing, God wot') must not be sent to Dr Dale. All last year's donors must be this

year's recipients, but once the known debts were honourably fulfilled, the real excitement of the season started. As cards, hair-tidies and markers began to arrive by every post they were checked against the list of out-going presents, and consternation reigned in Willow Lodge if it were found that Cousin Rose, who had sent a cut-glass vase, had been rewarded only by three coat-hangers in a cretonne case. Unexpected gifts sent the family ransacking drawers and cupboards to find suitable q.p.q.'s. (Beddows' jargon for quids pro quos.) The nearer the approach to Christmas Day itself, the lower ran the supply of possible exchanges, until finally even this year's presents were hastily repacked and despatched again hot from the post, with cards altered and brown paper readdressed.

Beside this transaction of civilities, there was the real business of benevolence to which all ready cash must be devoted – orders of beef to every Beddows ex-maid and her husband (and since all maids at Willow Lodge left to marry, the list was formidable), coals and blankets for ageing or invalid neighbours, toys, oranges, pennies and sweets for all the local children, and parcels of tea, cake and even whisky to dozens of often disreputable acquaintances who seemed to re-emerge in Mrs Beddows' consciousness only at Christmas time.

Nor was this all. To Willow Lodge at every season came beggars, derelicts, victims of domestic quarrels or economic injustices, the aged, infants and invalids; but between December 15 and January 5, the pilgrims doubled in number and desperation.

On the day before Christmas Eve Mrs Beddows had already interviewed a farm-worker whose wife was prematurely in labour, and for whom a nurse had to be found by persistent telephoning; a poultry-keeper, who had fled to Yorkshire after failures in the south, on whom the bailiffs had descended to seize incubators and hens against unpaid removal bills; an

elementary school teacher in trouble about the local Christmas Tree (which the squire had suddenly refused, on hearing that the Nonconformist children were to share it), and a mother who had just discovered that her schoolgirl daughter of sixteen was going to have a baby. Between the dining-room and the drawing-room Mrs Beddows trotted, resourceful, indefatigable and domineering.

'Well,' she exclaimed, 'we may be poor, but you can't say we don't see life.' She sighed.

'Here's a card from old Dr Menzies. Have we sent anything?'

Below it was an envelope marked 'Crown Hotel, Piccadilly,' and addressed to her in Carne's stiff squarish writing.

She opened that, frowning a little because Carne was not a correspondent, and she was expecting to see him next day when Midge returned to spend Christmas with her father.

'DEAR MRS BEDDOWS,' she read – 'I am writing to ask another favour of you.' He was almost the only man who used the long old-fashioned 'f' for 's'. 'I wonder if it would be very inconvenient to you to keep Midge on for Christmas? I know that she is very happy at Willow Lodge, and I fear that if she came to Maythorpe I could not give her the festive season which a child ought to have. Castle is very bad and things are not too good with me at present. I have been inquiring about accommodation here for my wife but have found nothing suitable.
    'Your ever grateful friend,

                                        'ROBT. CARNE.'

It was the longest letter that he had ever written her.

'Things are not too good with me.' Ah, well she knew it. Maythorpe mortgaged and the bank impatient, Snaith eager to buy the farm – for a mental home; Castle dying, Muriel no better. Carne had said that he would stick at Maythorpe till he

was forced off; he had said that he could last another year; but she knew that he had gone to Manchester to inquire about employment at a riding school there. He's too old, her heart cried. He's too old for that.

She remembered other Christmases at Maythorpe. Once in her childhood she had attended a dance there, when Robert's grandfather was master. She remembered the great decorated kitchen, with holly hung from the rafters among the salt-rimed shrouded hams and puddings, a fiddler on the back stairs, and a feast of cake and fruit and pasties, wine and whisky. Always there had been carol-singing on the drive, the square hall blazing with lights and pennies for the children. Until this year Robert had kept up some pretension of festivity. Now no more. He had cut down the timber except round the house itself; the rooms were untenanted by guests; the glory had departed.

Her only comfort was that in his extremity he could turn to her. He trusted her.

She held his letter, her longing to help and comfort him surging over her. 'Things are not too good with me.' It was the nearest approach to a complaint she had ever heard him make.

'Granny,' Peter broke into her reverie, 'you're wanted in the kitchen. The turkey's too big for the tin.'

'Let me go,' Sybil began.

'No. I will.'

Rousing herself, glad of the need for action, she levered her weary body from the deep chair, and hurried off.

It was nearly half an hour before she returned. The afternoon was waning, and the hall was almost dark. From the dining-room came a burst of light and laughter. It seemed to her, as she opened the door, to be full of people. A clamour of voices greeted her. Midge's shrill wild laugh, Peter's cackling shout (his voice was breaking), Wendy's glad guffaw, and another voice, deep and vibrating – Carne's voice.

While her hands and tongue were busy in the kitchen, she had been thinking of him with such love and sorrow that this unexpected re-encounter shocked her almost as though she had met a ghost. She had been thinking of his lonely Christmas, picturing him in the empty dining-room, eating his dinner alone with Muriel's portrait; she had been grieving over him, wondering what she could do to help him.

And now she saw him, seated by her fire, the centre of a delighted and boisterous uproar.

She could hardly believe her eyes.

He had brought his presents – a party dress of flowered silk for Midge, a hunting crop for Peter, a bracelet for Sybil, for Wendy a scarf of painted chiffon, for Jim a tie-pin with a fox's head, and for Willy a shagreen cigarette-box.

Midge saw her. 'Granny, come in. Come in! Look what Daddy's brought me!' She danced up and down, the rosy silk fluttering like a banner. Carne turned slowly and rose to greet her. Seen between those flushed excited faces his big dark figure seemed of other, different substance. He looks ill, she thought; he looks old. She began to reckon his age and decided that he must be fifty-three. He looks sixty. Oh, my dear, my poor one, what have they done to you?

'You've not come to fetch Midge away after all?' she asked.

He shook his head. The child sprang up and down.

'Oh, Granny, do say it suits me! Does it fit? Peter, don't crush it!'

'Look at my crop, Gran.'

'And look at this lovely thing.' Sybil held out a round, freckled arm with the gold bangle clasped on to it. Watching Carne's grave appreciation as he looked down at her pleasure, Emma Beddows thought, not for the first time – Oh, if he were free and could have married Sybil.

She moved towards him and began to inspect the presents. At first she thought he had gone crazy with extravagance.

Then she began to recognise one by one the bracelet, the scarf, the cigarette-box. These were his things and Muriel's. The former make-believe that she would return to use them was at an end.

'You'll stay for tea?'

'No. I've got to get back. Castle's bad to-night. I've promised to go round there.'

'Then you'll have a drink? Get him one, Sybil.'

'No, thank you very much.'

'Did you ride over?'

'No. I've got Hicks with the trap. I don't want to keep the horse waiting too long.'

'Then I'll come to the door with you.'

On her return from the kitchen, she had forgotten to remove her apron. Passing the mirror in the hall she saw reflected her plump, sturdy, plebeian figure beside his tall one, and sighed, desiring the impossible – that she could be young and lovely and desirable, that she could comfort him in his adversity.

He said, 'Is it all right about Midge?'

'Perfect for us, but you'll miss her.'

'I shall be all right.'

'Look here, why don't you come and eat your dinner with us?'

'I've promised to stand by Mrs Castle . . .'

'But . . .' She saw his resolution and changed the subject. 'How d'you think Midge is looking?'

'Splendid. This is the place for her. I – well – I wanted to ask you something.'

'What?'

She had opened the door. Its oblong was filled with the pale star-flecked radiance of the green evening sky. Hicks was leading his trap up and down the road outside the gate, its yellow lights crossing and turning beyond the dark laurel

hedge. Carne leaned against the door-post. She saw fatigue in all his slow calm gestures.

'I've been talking to my solicitors this morning,' he said, 'and I want to ask you a tremendous favour. Don't answer now. Think it over. If anything happened to me, would you be Midge's guardian?'

'But my dear boy! I'm seventy-two – old enough to be your mother.'

'I dare say. But you're young enough in some ways to be my daughter,' he said, and she could hear in his voice rather than read in his face his friendly grin. 'And I was nearly knocked down by a taxi in Manchester. It made me think of my latter end. If anything happened to me – the child would be rather lost. By the way, I've written to Sedgmire about Muriel.'

'Oh!'

Mrs Beddows realised what that implied.

'If I died, I expect they'd look after Muriel. They always would have done – if I'd leave her alone.' He tossed his cigarette on to the path. 'But Midge is a different matter. I don't want those Harrogate people to handle her.'

'Quite.'

'She wouldn't be any financial burden. I've kept up my insurance. Five thousand when I'm sixty or if I die before that. It's hers, of course. Only, I want to be sure I'm not putting too much on you.'

'No – no. I love the child. I'd do anything . . .'

'I know you would. That's just it. I exploit your goodness. I always have done.'

She could hardly breathe. Joy, release, triumph enfolded her.

'I don't think you know how fond I am of you,' she said.

'Perhaps I do.'

Hicks had turned the horse again; the dog-cart was approaching them, its lamps faint and small beside the great

lights of the passing motor-cars. In another moment this little interlude of tenderness would be over.

'By the way,' he added, 'that reminds me.' He fumbled in his waist-coat pocket and brought out a little box wrapped in tissue paper. 'I brought a little present for you too.'

'For me?'

'Yes. I want you to have it. You will know why. Goodbye. Merry Christmas to you.'

He took her hand, smiled, then very gravely stooped and kissed her soft wrinkled cheek and was off, out of the gate. She heard him call to Hicks; she saw the moving lights stop still; he climbed into the cart; he shook the reins, then the hoofs were off again, trot-trotting away from her into the starlight.

She put her hand to her face and touched it gently. He had never kissed her before. She had not dreamed of it. With trembling hands she began to undo her Christmas present. The paper contained a small brown case lined with white velvet, and on the velvet lay the brooch, a spray of emeralds, diamonds and rubies, which he had bought for Muriel when Midge was born. He had slipped into the lid a little card on which he had written, 'For Midge's Granny, in gratitude.'

'I want you to have it,' he had said. 'You will know why.' She knew why.

Here We Come a-Wassailing

A nineteenth-century carol from Yorkshire

Here we come a-wassailing
   Among the leaves so green,
Here we come a-wandering,
   So fair to be seen . . .

Love and joy come to you,
And to you your wassail too,

74

· A Yorkshire Christmas ·

And God bless you, and send you
A happy new year.

Our wassail cup is made
   Of the rosemary tree,
And so is your beer
   Of the best barley . . .

Call up the butler of this house,
   Put on his golden ring;
Let him bring us up a glass of beer,
   And better we shall sing . . .

God bless the master of this house,
   Likewise the mistress too;
And all the little children
   That round the table go . . .

Christmas
in Keighley
100 Years Ago

IAN DEWHIRST

Christmas Day in 1888 dawned frosty in Keighley, but rain
had set in by afternoon and made what the *Keighley News*

75

columnist, 'The Sparrow', called 'an umbrella Yule-tide'. Nevertheless, 'the turkey or goose', in the fervid journalistic style of the period, 'had no respite simply because the snow refused to fall'.

Not that snow was lacking in the imagination at least, being a popular ingredient in the repertoires of the many seasonal meals and entertainments. At the Amalgamated Society of Railway Servants' knife-and-fork tea at the Acorn Coffee Palace, a Miss Ackroyd sang 'Merrily, merrily, over the snow', while St Stephen's Church Sunday School at Steeton enjoyed a recitation called 'Beautiful Snow'.

But Keighley postmen were only too pleased to have 'got through their arduous Christmas labours all the more comfortably because of the absence of snow'. That Christmas, incidentally, they had delivered 25,000 cards and 2,000 parcels. The Rector, the Revd F.D. Cremer, and his wife, rewarded postmen and telegraph messengers with a breakfast at the Acorn, including cigars for the smokers and oranges for non-smokers.

Nearly everybody, it seems, got to a celebratory dinner or tea during the festive season. Keighley Spiritualists dined in Mr Weatherhead's Sale Rooms down Low Street. The Albert Street Baptists' repast was sternly linked with an address on 'A Church's Prosperity'. At Cowling, the United Methodists' scholars were assembled in their schoolroom by half-past seven in the morning on Christmas Day, but at least they were treated to cake after sitting through a talk. Later in the day, 500 sat down to tea.

Keighley firemen prudently took their hand hose-cart with them when they went to dine at the Devonshire Hotel, 'in case of a fire occurring while they were at dinner'. Unhappily, their meal was marred by a malicious false alarm from No. 14 box in Lawkholme Lane. After a wasted hour with their hose-cart and heavier appliances from the station, they resumed their

after-dinner songs and recitations, led by Captain Hotston who sang 'Tapping at the Window'.

The less fortunate were catered for. One hundred-and-thirty youngsters were treated to buns and cake at the Ragged School on Christmas Eve; Messrs Jonas Bottomley and Sons provided free sweets. One-hundred-and-eighty inmates of the workhouse and 64 patients in the infirmary had a Christmas dinner of roast beef and plum pudding, plus spice-cake and cheese for tea. Workhouse children were given presents off a Christmas tree. A well-wisher sent gifts to two lonely patients in the Keighley Cottage Hospital, including 'a zither harp for their solace'!

Even a solitary prisoner in the police cells received 'evidence of the season of goodwill in her dietary', while Bowcock's

Keighley Industrial Co-op, 1900

77

· *A Yorkshire Christmas* ·

Charity paid out a total of £231 to nearly 300 needy applicants.

If you had money to spend, 1888 offered plenty of scope. Thomas Frost, fish, game, poultry and fruit dealer of North Street, had stocked up with turkeys, geese, ducks, capons, grouse, hares, pheasants and venison, also poultry 'selected from the noted flocks of Norfolk, Surrey, Lincolnshire, and Cambridgeshire'; he specialised too in 'finest Whitstable, Dutch, and other oysters'.

The Market offered a 'great show of Christmas beef' and boasted an illuminated Prince of Wales feathers at its main entrance.

Places of worship were decorated for their carol services, the still-new St Peter's in Halifax Road being singled out for description, with its 'neatly-finished designs and wreaths done

'Shovelling Snow' – caption given by the photographer, Amos Dewhirst, to this group of children at the back of his tobacconist and newsagent shop in Keighley, 1905

78

in holly, laurel, box, and ivy, together with several appropriate texts and the addition of choice flowers'.

At St Peter's they combined their carol service with a distribution of Lord Wharton Bibles, whilst for theirs Keighley Parish Church secured the talents of the highly qualified organist from Halifax Parish Church. At Silsden, 'pleasing and suitable selections' were played by the brass band.

Secular entertainment was not lacking. Marriner's Brass Band led the dancing at Keighley Drill Hall on Christmas Eve. Citizens melodramatically inclined could see *Wronged, or Through the Furnace* at the Mechanics' Institute. The Queen's Theatre was presenting 'an entirely new realistic and sensational comedy-drama' called *Light o' Day* – since this purported to expose 'the evils of the Lunacy and Poor Laws', the comedy element would appear to have been somewhat stretched.

Presumably the theatre management thought *Light o' Day* unsuitable for Christmas Day itself: on 25th December they offered two grand variety smoking concerts instead!

Captain Cook's Christmases

James Cook was born in Marton, Yorkshire, in 1728 and moved soon afterwards to the village of Great Ayton, where he went to school. His house is not there now, having been

intense as hardly to be endured, the whole sea in a manner covered with ice, a hard gale and a thick fog. Under all these unfavourable circumstances it was natural for me to think of returning more to the north.

On Cook's death in Hawaii, the surgeon's mate on board the *Resolution* wrote:

Nature had endowed him with a mind vigorous and comprehensive, which in his riper years he had cultivated with care and industry. His general knowledge was extensive and various: in that of his own profession he was unequalled. With a clear judgment, strong masculine sense, and the most determined resolution: with a genius peculiarly turned for enterprise, he pursued his object with unshaken perseverance – vigilant and active in an eminent degree: cool and intrepid among dangers: patient and firm under difficulties and distress: fertile in expedients: great and original in all his designs: active and resolved in carrying them into execution. In every situation he stood unrivalled and alone: on him all eyes were turned: he was our leading star, which at its setting left us involved in darkness and despair.

from

Wuthering Heights

EMILY BRONTË

Cathy stayed at Thrushcross Grange five weeks: till Christmas. By that time her ankle was thoroughly cured, and her manners much improved: so that, instead of a wild, hatless little savage jumping into the house, and rushing to squeeze us all breathless, there alighted from a handsome black pony a very dignified person, with brown ringlets falling from the cover of a feathered beaver, and a long cloth habit, which she was obliged to hold up with both hands that she might sail in. Hindley lifted her from her horse, exclaiming delightedly, 'Why, Cathy, you are quite a beauty! I should scarcely have known you; you look like a lady now.'

'But she must mind, and not grow wild again here,' replied his wife. 'Ellen, help Miss Catherine off with her things; stay, dear, you will disarrange your curls — let me untie your hat.'

I removed the habit, and there shone forth beneath, a grand plaid silk frock, white trousers, and burnished shoes. She kissed me gently, and then she looked round for Heathcliff.

Heathcliff was hard to discover at first. If he were careless and uncared for before Catherine's absence, he had been ten times more so since. Nobody but I even did him the kindness to call him a dirty boy, and bid him wash himself, once a week; and children of his age seldom have a natural pleasure in soap and

83

water. He might well skulk behind the settle, on beholding such a bright, graceful damsel enter the house, instead of a rough-headed counterpart of himself, as he expected.

'Is Heathcliff not here?' she demanded, pulling off her gloves, and displaying fingers wonderfully whitened with doing nothing and staying indoors.

'Heathcliff, you may come forward,' cried Mr Hindley, enjoying his discomfiture, and gratified to see what a forbidding young blackguard he would be compelled to present himself. 'You may come and wish Miss Catherine welcome, like the other servants.'

Cathy, catching a glimpse of her friend, in his concealment, flew to embrace him; she bestowed seven or eight kisses on his cheek within the second, and then stopped, and drawing back, burst into a laugh, exclaiming –

'Why, how very black and cross you look! and how – how funny and grim! But that's because I'm used to Edgar and Isabella Linton. Well, Heathcliff, have you forgotten me?'

She had some reason to put the question, for shame and pride threw double gloom over his countenance, and kept him immovable.

'Shake hands, Heathcliff,' said Mr Earnshaw condescendingly; 'once in a way, that is permitted.'

'I shall not,' replied the boy, finding his tongue at last; 'I shall not stand to be laughed at. I shall not bear it!' And he would have broken from the circle, but Miss Cathy seized him again.

'I did not mean to laugh at you,' she said; 'I could not hinder myself; Heathcliff, shake hands at least! What are you sulky for? It was only that you looked odd. If you wash your face and brush your hair, it will be all right; but you are so dirty!'

With that he dashed head-foremost out of the room, amid the merriment of the master and mistress, and to the serious

disturbance of Catherine; who could not comprehend how her remarks should have produced such an exhibition of bad temper.

After playing lady's-maid to the new-comer, and putting my cakes in the oven, and making the house and kitchen cheerful with great fires, befitting Christmas Eve, I prepared to sit down and amuse myself by singing carols all alone; regardless of Joseph's affirmations that he considered the merry tunes I chose as next door to songs.

Mr and Mrs Earnshaw had invited the little Lintons to spend the morrow at Wuthering Heights, and the invitation had been accepted, on one condition; Mrs Linton begged that her darlings might be kept carefully apart from that 'naughty swearing boy.'

Under these circumstances I remained solitary. I smelled the rich scent of the heating spices; and admired the shining kitchen utensils and the polished clock, decked in holly. I gave due inward applause to every object, and then I remembered how old Earnshaw used to come in when all was tidied, and call me a cant lass, and slip a shilling into my hand as a Christmas-box; and from that I went on to think of his fondness for Heathcliff, and his dread lest he should suffer neglect after death had removed him; and that naturally led me to consider the poor lad's situation now, and from singing I changed my mind to crying. It struck me soon, however, there would be more sense in endeavouring to repair some of his wrongs than shedding tears over them; I got up and walked into the court to seek him. He was not far; I found him smoothing the glossy coat of the new pony in the stable, and feeding the other beasts according to custom.

'Make haste, Heathcliff!' I said, 'the kitchen is so comfortable, and Joseph is upstairs.'

He proceeded with his task, and never turned his head towards me.

'Come – are you coming?' I continued. 'There's a little cake for each of you, nearly enough; and you'll need half an hour's donning.'

I waited five minutes, but getting no answer left him. Catherine supped with her brother and sister-in-law; Joseph and I joined at an unsociable meal, seasoned with reproofs on one side and sauciness on the other. His cake and cheese remained on the table all night for the fairies. He managed to continue work till nine o'clock, and then marched dumb and dour to his chamber. Cathy sat up late, having a world of things to order for the reception of her new friends; she came into the kitchen once to speak to her old one; but he was gone, and she only stayed to ask what was the matter with him, and then went back. In the morning he rose early; and, as it was a holiday, carried his ill-humour on to the moors; not reappearing till the family were departed for church.

Fasting and reflection seemed to have brought him to a better spirit. He hung about me for a while, and having screwed up his courage, exclaimed abruptly –

'Nelly, make me decent; I'm going to be good.'

'High time, Heathcliff,' I said; 'you *have* grieved Catherine: she's sorry she ever came home.'

'Did you say she was grieved?' he inquired, looking very serious.

'She cried when I told her you were off again this morning.'

'Well, *I* cried last night,' he returned; 'and I had more reason to cry than she.'

'Yes; you had the reason of going to bed with a proud heart and an empty stomach,' said I. 'Proud people breed sad sorrows for themselves. But, if you be ashamed of your touchiness, you must ask pardon, mind, when she comes in. You must go up and offer to kiss her, and say – you know best what to say; only do it heartily, and not as if you thought her converted into a stranger by her grand dress. And now, though

I have dinner to get ready, I'll steal time to arrange you so that Edgar Linton shall look quite a doll beside you: and that he does. You are younger, and yet, I'll be bound, you are taller and twice as broad across the shoulders; you could knock him down in a twinkling, don't you feel that you could?'

Heathcliff's face brightened a moment; then it was overcast afresh, and he sighed.

'But, Nelly, if I knocked him down twenty times, that wouldn't make him less handsome or me more so. I wish I had light hair and a fair skin, and was dressed and behaved as well, and had a chance of being as rich as he will be!'

'And cried for mamma at every turn,' I added, 'and trembled if a country lad heaved his fist against you, and sat at home all day for a shower of rain. Oh, Heathcliff, you are showing a poor spirit! Were I in your place, I would frame high notions of my birth; and the thoughts of what I was should give me courage and dignity to support the oppressions of a little farmer!'

So I chattered on, and Heathcliff gradually lost his frown and began to look quite pleasant, when all at once our conversation was interrupted by a rumbling sound moving up the road and entering the court. He ran to the window and I to the door, just in time to behold the two Lintons descend from the family carriage, smothered in cloaks and furs, and the Earnshaws dismount from their horses; they often rode to church in winter. Catherine took a hand of each of the children, and brought them into the house and set them before the fire, which quickly put colour into their white faces.

I urged my companion to hasten now and show his amiable humour, and he willingly obeyed; but ill luck would have it that, as he opened the door leading from the kitchen on one side, Hindley opened it on the other. They met, and the master, irritated at seeing him clean and cheerful – or, perhaps, eager to keep his promise to Mrs Linton – shoved him

back with a sudden thrust, and angrily bade Joseph 'keep the fellow out of the room – send him into the garret till dinner is over. He'll be cramming his fingers in the tarts and stealing the fruit, if let alone with them a minute.'

'Nay, sir,' I could not avoid answering, 'he'll touch nothing, not he; and I suppose he must have his share of the dainties as well as we.'

'He shall have his share of my hand, if I catch him downstairs till dark,' cried Hindley. 'Begone, you vagabond! What! you are attempting the coxcomb, are you? Wait till I get hold of those elegant locks – see if I won't pull them a bit longer!'

'They are long enough already,' observed Master Linton, peeping from the doorway; 'I wonder they don't make his head ache. It's a colt's mane over his eyes!'

He ventured this remark without any intention to insult; but Heathcliff's violent nature was not prepared to endure the appearance of impertinence from one whom he seemed to hate, even then, as a rival. He seized a tureen of hot apple sauce, the first thing that came under his grip, and dashed it full against the speaker's face and neck; who instantly commenced a lament that brought Isabella and Catherine hurrying to the place. Mr Earnshaw snatched up the culprit directly and conveyed him to his chamber; where, doubtless, he administered a rough remedy to cool the fit of passion, for he appeared red and breathless. I got the dish-cloth, and rather spitefully scrubbed Edgar's nose and mouth, affirming it served him right for meddling. His sister began weeping to go home, and Cathy stood by confounded, blushing for all.

'You should not have spoken to him!' she expostulated with Master Linton. 'He was in a bad temper, and now you've spoiled your visit; and he'll be flogged: I hate him to be flogged! I can't eat my dinner. Why did you speak to him, Edgar?'

'I didn't,' sobbed the youth, escaping from my hands, and finishing the remainder of the purification with his cambric pocket-handkerchief. 'I promised mamma that I wouldn't say one word to him, and I didn't.'

'Well, don't cry,' replied Catherine contemptuously. 'You're not killed. Don't make more mischief; my brother is coming: be quiet! Hush! Isabella! Has anybody hurt *you?*'

'There, there, children – to your seats!' cried Hindley, bustling in. 'That brute of a lad has warmed me nicely. Next time, Master Edgar, take the law into you own fists – it will give you an appetite!'

The little party recovered its equanimity at sight of the fragrant feast. They were hungry after their ride, and easily consoled, since no real harm had befallen them. Mr Earnshaw carved bountiful platefuls, and the mistress made them merry with lively talk. I waited behind her chair, and was pained to behold Catherine with dry eyes, and an indifferent air, commence cutting up the wing of a goose before her.

She lifted a mouthful to her lips; then she set it down again; her cheeks flushed, and the tears gushed over them. She slipped her fork to the floor, and hastily dived under the cloth to conceal her emotion. I did not call her unfeeling long; for I perceived she was in purgatory throughout the day, and wearying to find an opportunity of getting by herself, or paying a visit to Heathcliff – who had been locked up by the master – as I discovered, on endeavouring to introduce to him a private mess of victuals.

In the evening we had a dance. Cathy begged that he might be liberated then, as Isabella Linton had no partner; her entreaties were vain, and I was appointed to supply the deficiency. We got rid of all gloom in the excitement of the exercise, and our pleasure was increased by the arrival of the Gimmerton band, mustering fifteen strong – a trumpet, a trombone, clarionets, bassoons, French horns, and a bass viol,

besides singers. They go the rounds of all the respectable houses, and receive contributions every Christmas, and we esteemed it a first-rate treat to hear them. After the usual carols had been sung, we set them to songs and glees. Mrs Earnshaw loved the music, and so they gave us plenty.

from

The Leeds Christmas Book

P. BREARS

The Mummers

The mummers were parties of juveniles who went about several weeks before Christmas, and during the week, acting the play of St. George in the public houses. They, in number eight or nine, were decked out in coloured calico, tinselled, tinned and ribboned, according to the taste of their respective materfamilias, who took great interest in the matter, which, with a helmet, either of pasteboard, tin, or stiffened calico, and a weapon, called a sword, completed their equipment.

The play was generally known as *The Peace Egg* from its

being performed at Easter (and was therefore paschal) in other localities. In its dramatic action, St. George, the patron saint of England, proceeded to defeat Slasher, the Black Prince of Paradine, and Hector, before Devil Doubt arrived to demand money from the audience.

Devil Doubt of course was well sooted (as were the Moors), carried a besom with him, and where practical, a tail. There were numbers of these mummers early last century, consisting principally of those employed in the textile mills.

Pantomime

By the mid-nineteenth century the various theatres and music halls of Leeds were able to offer a wealth of entertainment for the Christmas season. In 1866, for example, there was ballet at the West Riding Concert Hall in Kirkgate, a 'Gorgeous Christmas Revel' at Thornton's Music Hall and Theatre of Varieties, Headrow, 'Gonysetz's Spectroscope' at the Stock Exchange, Albion Street, and 'Grand Historical Equestrian scenes and Brilliant Spectacles' at Newsome's Grand Circus, Cookridge Street. At the Princess Concert Hall, King Charles' Croft, even more impressive scenes could be witnessed, including 'a Fairy Spectacular Entertainment on a scale of splendour never before attempted out of London, introducing a magnificent water scene entitled "The Titanic Cascades of Real Water and Sports of Fairy Land" . . .'

Despite this considerable competition, the real triumph of the season appears to have been the pantomime promoted by Mr Loraine, lessee and manager of the Royal Amphitheatre, King Charles' Croft. Entitled *Sinbad the Sailor, or the Giant Ogre! The Red Dwarfs, and the Old Man of the Sea*, its climax was a vast transformation scene utilising a wealth of stage machinery and special effects.

'When the curtain rises we see a bed of coral, over which hang festoons of seaweed and stalactite. The former slowly

91

descend and the latter rise and part, and gradually fairy forms, enveloped in gold and silver tissue, appear upon the scene, some reclining within shells gorgeously illuminated by variegated lights, others suspended in mid air, while one radiant creature in a robe of dazzling splendour ascends slowly to the sound of soft music, on the summit of a vast globe of burnished silver, at the base of which groups of fairies lie clustered. The whole, illuminated up by electric light and coloured fires, forms a scene of marvellous beauty. The applause it excited was most enthusiastic and the audience redoubled their demonstrations when Mr Loraine complied with their summons, and reminded them that he had promised them a good pantomime.'

Over the following years pantomimes were staged at most of the major Leeds theatres, including the Grand and the Queen's, but it was at the Theatre Royal (built on the site of the Amphitheatre in 1876) that Francis Laidler developed the most successful pantomime tradition in northern England. Each year, from 1909 to 1957, the Theatre Royal pantomimes were so popular that they ran for up to 22 weeks, far beyond their original Christmas season.

Now most of the old Leeds theatres have been demolished, and those which remain are unable to provide the spectacle and grandeur of the pantomimes of last century.

Christmas at the Vicarage

Probably no parish church in England can boast of such a fine musical tradition as that maintained at St Peter's in Kirkgate. This is largely due to the work of Dean Hook, the great reforming Vicar of Leeds.

When he came in 1837 the church was dilapidated with the surplices in rags and the service books in tatters. By 1841 he had changed everything beyond recognition, the church itself having been handsomely rebuilt, with a new peal of bells and a

· A Yorkshire Christmas ·

'The "Stand-back Slasher" boys rehearse their parts'

'The toper anticipates the festive season'

'The Christmas Martyr'

'Mr Jinks essays to acquire the art of waltzing in the privacy of his bedroom'

'The concertina fiend awakes the echoes'

'The shadows of pantomime come in view'

Christmas characters in Leeds, 1881

newly rebuilt organ. The quality of the church music was similarly improved, the composer Samuel Sebastian Wesley serving as organist, and Mr James Hill of Her Majesty's Chapel Royal, Windsor, leading the choir of 35 voices. Full choral services were now introduced for all weekday evenings, in addition to those for Sundays and Holy days.

Samuel Dyer was one of the choirboys at this time, and he has recorded the festivities which Dean Hook organised for the choir at the vicarage at No. 6, Park Place.

'At Christmas we all dined, men and boys, at the vicarage: grand for us boys. Plum-pudding, roast beef, and the games of hunting for sixpences in hillocks of flour, turned out of a basin, or bobbing for apples dangling from a string; after that, presents of knives and books . . . Before breaking up we had rounds, glees and madrigals, "Old Thomas Day," "Great Tom is Cast."

'For several nights about X'mastide we trudged to the suburban seats to sing outside the mansions of the gentry who frequented the Parish Church, for which we reaped a rich harvest.'

Messiah

The West Riding of Yorkshire has a unique choral tradition in which oratorio has always played a leading part. For over two centuries the choirs of churches, chapels and choral societies throughout the county have regularly celebrated their Christmas season with performances of Handel's masterpiece, *Messiah*, constantly striving for the highest standards.

'On September 9th, 1768, "Messiah", a sacred oratorio compos'd by Mr Handel will begin in the Assembly Room and will be repeated every other Friday night throughout the winter, being 18 nights,' announced the *Leeds Mercury*. From that time there have been performances in the city almost every year, many being held in the Town Hall's imposing Victoria Hall.

· A Yorkshire Christmas ·

In December 1976 the Victoria Hall witnessed one of the most spontaneous and exciting *Messiahs*. Radio Leeds had assembled a thousand members of the public who wanted to sing their respective parts, together with a volunteer orchestra of sixty. As the producer commented, 'What resulted was an amazing and unique sound. Whether it was panic, adrenalin, or sheer exhilaration, it was the most moving experience many had witnessed.' 'Come and sing *Messiah*' has proved so popular, that it now shows every sign of becoming an established tradition in its own right.

Christmas in the Mills

In the 1840s the young Steward Tempest worked as a 'half-timer' at Armley Mills, one half of his working day being spent in the manufacture of woollen cloth, while the other was spent in the mill school. Later in life, when he was operating his own company in the mills, he remembered how Mr Gott, the mill owner, always came to give presents to his staff at Christmas time. The workforce lined both sides of the steep stone staircase within Armley Mills, and proceeded to sing carols, after which Mr Gott passed down between them, distributing suitable sums to each person in turn as their Christmas box.

Christmas Day in the Workhouse

In 1860 the Leeds Board of Guardians completed the New Workhouse in Burmantofts, this large building in the Eliza-bethan style housing 848 of the city's poor. Life in the workhouse was far from pleasant, but on Christmas days, 'both the establishment and its character were changed. Where stern order usually ruled, supervised by naked gauntness, the emblems of mirth were evident. To the inmates of the Workhouse proper dinner was served in the large dining hall,

95

looking bright and cheerful with mottoes, texts, designs and festoons. Close upon 470 men and women had a dinner of roast beef and plum pudding with coffee at the close. By the hearty appetites of the diners there were disposed of 46 stones of beef, 6 of suet, 37 of potatoes, and the pudding contained 100 lb of plums, 50 lb of currants and 40 lb of sultanas. Sweets and tobacco came afterwards, and an entertainment of a "free and easy" character appropriately ended an enjoyable day.'

The Way We Were

R. W. SCALES

Ron Scales, as a native of Pickering, has always had a keen interest in its evolution. With the help of the staff of Pickering Library, and after talking to senior citizens and delving into old newspapers, he has produced his own version of 'The Way We Were'.

1857 *Christmas Holidays* The shopkeepers of Pickering this year gave their apprentices a holiday from Thursday evening to Monday the 28th ult: and we have no doubt but such kindness will be returned by a strict attention to their master's business and interests.

1859 *Church Singers* Mr Cockburn the vicar has decided

upon having no more paid singers in the church. Owing to that decision the present singers have struck and for the past two Sundays have not attended. Dr Camidge from York has been instructed to attend to teach a new choir.

1859 *13th December* *Snow Storm* We had a very frosty day and in the evening a most terrific storm of snow from the north west, the frost being most intense. On the 14th the wind blew a complete hurricane, the roads being drifted up and in many places impassable. In the afternoon the snow fell thickly and fast and the drifts rose rapidly. Many travellers were stopped and obliged to remain all night at roadside inns. The Rosedale and Lastingham post passengers were much distressed in the snow, Mr Ellis suffering severely on the moor and having a narrow escape from being lost. We have not had a worse storm for many years.

1859 *24th December* During the past few days the weather has been most wintry, the frost being more severe than has

Midwife stranded, Lockton, 1947

been remembered for many years back. The Pickering High Mill and several others are frozen up, likewise the railway engine on Sunday was brought to a stop by the frost and could not proceed until thawed.

1859 *Generosity* Colonel Mitchelson, previous to Christmas Day, slaughtered a beast and gave it to the poor of Pickering. Matthew Monkman Esq of Pickering also distributed a quarter of beef amongst the poor. Such kind feelings for the poor at this season of the year is worthy of the greatest praise.

1865 *January* On the 4th inst: a son of Mr W. Tute of Pickering had his hand bit through by a large dog. This is not the first time this dog has bit people and it is high time it was destroyed or kept secure.

Caution to Skaters On Friday last whilst a young man named Wm. Barraclough was skating on a large sheet of water

Reg Harvey, the UDC Foreman, at Pickering

known as Narvey Hole near to the coal depot Pickering, the ice broke and he fell through but fortunately escaped with a cold bath. This is the second accident at this place within a week.

Benevolence   During the late severe weather Mr John Carr, Market Place, Pickering gave to his tenants and the destitute poor, one stone of flour each. Such kindness is worthy of imitation.

1867   *January   Grand Dress Ball*   The Sax-Horn Band gave their first grand dress ball on New Year's Eve in Mr Frank's Assembly Room which was very well attended by persons from Scarborough, Whitby, and Pickering considering the stormy night. The dancing was kept up with animation by Mr Harker's Quadrille Band and the refreshments were provided by Mrs Frank of the Kings Arms.

1867   *January*   Two miners making their way from Scarborough to Rosedale got 'bogged' in a snow gully in Crosscliffe when they were unable to get out. The men remained all night in the snow and were found nearly starved to death next morning, and not at all aware where they were.

1868   *January*   The Agricultural Gang Act came into operation on Wednesday week. The Act prohibits the employment of children under 8 years of age in agricultural labour and also enforces a separation of the sexes in field work.

1869   *January*   Isabel Scales aged 13 years was charged with attempting to poison Mr and Mrs Dodsworth, their 3 children and 2 servant boys at Pickering Marishes by administering Tartar Emetic and Saltpetre kept to give to a horse that was unwell. The prisoner said that she did it because the boys 'skelped and bunched' her. She was found guilty, but the

judge took a merciful view of her crime and found her guilty of misdemeanour and sentenced her to one day's imprisonment.

1869 *December Thunderstorms* The North Riding rivers have risen rapidly and there is every appearance of an overflow. Near Stape a man with a pony and cart was overtaken by the storm. The cart was shattered to pieces by the lightning and the pony thrown some distance. A large hole was left in the road on the spot, the driver who was some distance behind escaped unhurt.

1870 *January Seasonable Benevolence* During the late very inclement weather the Wesleyans of Pickering, in a spirit of charity and liberality, announced their intention of providing soup and bread to be given without distinction of sex or creed to all poor persons in Pickering. This was carried out in a praiseworthy manner, each recipient getting a quart of excellent soup, gratis and a 2d loaf for which latter the sum of one penny was paid.

1871 The Primitive Methodists of Pickering have set an excellent example for the guidance of religious bodies in Pickering. Remembering that it is more blessed to give than to receive, they have given 15 stones of coals to above 100 widows and poor families irrespective of creed. A more seasonable gift hardly would have been given than coals this inclement weather.

1871 *December* On Christmas Day the train from Whitby, due at Pickering at 7 pm, ran through the station without stopping. The gatekeeper of the level crossing at the bottom of the Market Place had got one gate open and the other one partly open when the engine dashed up and smashed the gate to pieces, the gatekeeper, James Hunter, escaped without injury.

· A Yorkshire Christmas ·

1875 *January*   Winter has set in with severity this year and Christmas was one of the old fashioned sort. Every day for the last 12 or 14 days snow has fallen in considerable quantities and the average depth now varies from about 10 to 18 inches but in many places it is a yard or more in depth. The cold has been intense and Pickering Beck is frozen enough for sliding and skating, a circumstance which has not occurred for many years. Those who like Christmas weather at Christmas time have had it in abundance.

Christmas Festivities at Pickering   During the whole of Christmas week the weather was so intensely cold that few people ventured out of their homes, but on Christmas Eve several bands of singers went round the town. On Saturday R.P. Clarkson Esq of Pickering provided for the whole of his workmen and their wives and a number of friends, an excellent dinner consisting of roast and boiled beef, turkey, goose and giblet pie and plum pudding etc., to which ample justice was done. The 29 men employed at Mr Chadwick's limestone quarries, Pickering received 5/- each from their employer as a Christmas Box.

Whitby Road, Great Blizzard, 1933

· A Yorkshire Christmas ·

1879 The poor of Pickering were not forgotten this festive season, J.M. Mitchelson Esq of the Hall and M. Monkman Esq, on Christmas Eve, with their usual liberality had killed a fat beast and distributed it among the deserving poor. The shop windows were all temptingly dressed and the evening was beautifully clear, frosty and moonlit. At midnight the church bells rang out a merry peal, during the whole night bands of singers perambulated the town singing before the houses of their various friends. The streets were thronged all night, the rough elements being predominate. The new Temperance Coffee shop was kept open all night and did a good trade. Next day the inmates of the Workhouse had a capital dinner of roast beef and plum pudding provided for them, with gifts for all. During the afternoon the skating rink at the High Mill was well patronised by the young people of the town.

1882 *December The Storm* There was a heavy fall of snow on Tuesday night and all day on Wednesday. The storm raged fearfully and never before was anything like it witnessed in this district. There were drifts of snow at Lastingham from 7 to 9 feet high and at Lockton, Levisham, Thornton, Allerston, Wilton and Brawby still greater in height. All trains were delayed and an additional engine had to be attached to all trains up to Whitby, between Pickering and Rosedale Abbey there were wagons and all sorts of vehicles snowed up, one of the rural postmen had a narrow escape from being buried in the snow.

Death from Exposure Michael Ventress of Horcum near Saltersgate died from exposure to the storm on Wednesday night. The funeral of the deceased took place on Sunday and on the previous day the able bodied men of Lockton and Levisham were arduously engaged in cutting a track to the churchyard. The immense blocks of snow that had to be cut away was a work that entailed incessant toil. The funeral procession

102

presented a sad and singular appearance as the mourners wended their way to the burial ground, immense walls of ice encompassing them on each side.

1884 *January* *The King of Tramps* At the Police Court on Wednesday, George Scott was brought up and charged with begging at Pickering on the previous day. The prisoner had on four coats and two vests and attached to one of the coats were two rings and a thimble denoting him to be the King of Tramps, and on another were 78 buttons which denoted his age, whilst on a third he had buttons of all nations and several belonging to various police forces and one which he prized most of all was dated 1713 from the Cheltenham day schools. The number of buttons on this coat denoted the number of days in the year. He also had in his possession a large quantity of buttons of all descriptions and a wooden spoon which he stated came from Beverley gaol. The prisoner was severely cautioned and on promising to leave the town, was discharged.

1886 *January* *Seasonable Benevolence* During the past few weeks the poor of Pickering have been exceedingly well cared for, the gentry of the district having this year displayed their hospitality in an almost unprecedented measure. In order to provide the poorer classes with a substantial Christmas dinner, Mr J.M. Mitchelson of the Hall slaughtered two fine beasts and with his usual liberality distributed useful pieces of beef amongst the deserving poor. Mr T. Mitchelson also gave a quantity of beef and Messrs Sterricker contributed liberally in the same direction as did also Mr J. Kitching, Mr J. Watson, Mr J. Frank, Mr Thos. Frank and other gentlemen. As soon as the severe weather set in and a number of agricultural and other labourers were, in consequence, deprived of their work, a meeting of the principal residents of the town raised a subscription for distributing coals and soup.

1888 *December Saucy Vagrants* At the court house on Tuesday two vagrants named Wilson and Smith were charged with destroying their clothing whilst in the vagrant ward of the Pickering Workhouse. The workhouse master found them on Monday morning naked, their clothing and boots being cut to pieces, each was sent to Northallerton gaol for one month.

1895 *January* Watch Night Services were held at the various places of worship on New Year's Eve. The heavy snow put a stop to all the outdoor demonstrations. On Tuesday morning the mail carts to Helmsley and Rosedale were unable to accomplish their journeys owing to the drifted state of the roads, the Rosedale letters being brought back to Pickering and remained there until Wednesday morning, while those for Helmsley had to be forwarded by train.

1900 *The War* We understand that 14 or 15 of the best shots in the Pickering Volunteer Corps have volunteered for active service in South Africa.

January A Row at the Workhouse George Barker and Thomas Goodwill, 69 years and 76 years old respectively, were charged with being 'disorderly paupers'; they had quarrelled over breaking cinders and it ended in a fight. The bench said it was a serious offence but as they had been locked up for one night they would look over it this time, if they were brought before the court again they would be severely dealt with.

December Christmas services were held in most places of worship on Christmas Day, the festive morn was ushered in by the playing of two local bands, Skaife's and the Old Town Band, the church choir visited the Hall and sang in other parts of the town. The waits went their usual rounds and in the evening of Christmas Day a sacred Cantata *David* was given in the Independent Chapel. The inmates of the Workhouse were again allowed their customary Christmas dinner of roast beef

Top shop at Rosedale, *c.* 1910

and plum pudding and were not forgotten by outside friends who sent gifts of oranges, apples, sweets, tea, sugar, nuts, grapes, tobacco, etc. Dr Robertson and Mr F.H. Sterricker carved the beef which was a prime cut of about 5 stones from Mr G. Barber's prize beef.

1906 *January* Jas Hill, farmer of Marishes, was fined 2/6d and costs for being drunk and disorderly on December 11th 1905. The clerk asked the defendant if he had any questions to put to the witness. Defendant 'No sir, if he (meaning the PC) says I was drunk, I must have been.'

1907 *December* *Pickering Board of Guardians* At a meeting, among other things, a bottle of Brandy was asked for, this was stated to be for the sauce. Mr Marwood proposed that it was not allowed, he did without it himself, Mr Coverdale seconded. Mr J. Creaser 'We are getting a bit grubby by gum' and proposed they allow the brandy, Mr Ed Frank seconded. The vote was 9 to 7 against, and it was disallowed.

1914 *January Death of Mr F.H. Sterricker* In 1879 he founded his establishment for the breeding of carriage horses and hackneys, and since 1892 he has supplied State Coach horses to the King of Italy and to the President of the Argentine, as well as to Australia, Belgium, South Africa, France, Germany, Denmark, Sweden, Mexico, Canada, Russia and Holland.

1915 *December Pickering Provision Market* Prices of Christmas Poultry were as follows: Turkeys (undressed) 11d and 1/- per lb, Geese (dressed) 10½d per lb, Ducks (dressed) 11½d to 1/- per lb, Chickens (dressed) 3/6d to 3/9d each, Butter 1/6d per lb, Eggs 5 for 1/-, Rabbits 2/2d to 2/4d couple, Hares 3/- to 3/9d each.

Cromwell's Christmas Victory at Skipton

Four days before Christmas in 1645, Lady Anne Clifford instructed Sir John Mallory and 300 soldiers to lay down their arms and surrender Skipton Castle to Cromwell's superior forces. So ended a disastrous year for the forces of Charles I.

The history of Skipton is a long one, and prosperity only really came to the town when the castle was built, after the Norman invasion. Before that it had been a hamlet inhabited by Angles, who reputedly named it 'Sceptone', meaning 'Sheep town'.

The castle itself has a varied history. Prior to the Norman invasion the large estate, comprising nineteen hamlets of which Skipton was one, belonged to Edwin of Mercia, a Saxon Earl, whose Manor House was at 'Bodeltone', near the present site of Bolton Priory. But his lands were confiscated by William the Conqueror following the defeat of the Northern army in 1068.

In 1138 William FitzDuncan, the nephew of David, King of Scotland, laid waste much of the North of England, and later the Scots destroyed Skipton Castle. Alice de Romille, the heiress to the castle and Honour of Skipton, became William FitzDuncan's bride in 1152, and their daughter later married the Earl of Albermarle. The castle and lands remained the possession of the Earls of Albermarle until 1245, then became a Crown possession. In 1310 the famous de Clifford family moved to Skipton as protectors against the Scots, and remained until 1675.

The first Lord Clifford began building the present castle early in the fourteenth century, in compliance with Edward I's wishes that the castle resume a military role to combat repeated Scottish raids, and it was largely completed by the mid-fourteenth century. Several of its Lords, however, were subsequently killed on foreign battlefields. A century later, in the Wars of the Roses, Skipton Castle supported the Lancastrians! The 9th Lord Clifford, only twenty-six, met his death at the bloodbath of Towton Field in 1461. History and Shakespeare called him 'Black Clifford, the Butcher', because he was said to have slain in cold blood the Duke of York's young son and, having removed the head of the Duke himself, taken it to Margaret of Anjou, Henry VI's wife, on a pike! Skipton supported Elizabeth I during 'The Rising of the North' in the late sixteenth century, and in 1642 was besieged by Cromwell's forces.

Sir John Mallory and his 300 men held the castle for three years for Lady Anne Clifford, but eventually surrendered on 21 December 1645. The severe damage that Cromwell's forces inflicted on the building was repaired by Lady Anne Clifford between 1650 and her death in 1676, and it is to her careful restoration work that the castle owes its appearance today. In spite of being a diminutive woman only 4 ft 10 in tall, she had an abundance of energy, so that in the last fifteen years of her life, with Charles II's approval, she restored all her ancient possessions to their former splendour – castles, churches and houses ravaged by the Civil War. She was loved by the people of the Dales and perhaps her finest epitaph is the one they spoke on her death:

'She was last 'on 'em, and best o't' lot.'

The Death of Robin Hood

EDWARD BAINES

Kirklees is famous as the occasional residence and sepulchre of that ancient archer and freebooter, Robin Hood, who lived at the beginning of the thirteenth century, and who, according to tradition, was suffered to bleed to death by a nun, to whom he had applied to take from him a portion of his redundant blood. That such a character existed, the testimony of Piers Ploughman appears to decide; whether he was, as the epitaph preserved by Dr Gale, Dean of York, imports, of noble parentage, or an outlaw of humbler birth, is not equally clear; but that his mortal remains rest at Kirklees, under an ancient cross, and beyond the precincts of the nunnery, is generally admitted. The cross bears no inscription, but the epitaph may have been engraved upon a tomb-stone, which has ceased to exist: it is in these words:

> Hear, undernead dis latil stean,
> Laiz Robert, Earl of Huntington;
> Nea areir vir as him sa geud,
> An pipl kauld him Robin Heud;
> Sick utlauz az hi, an iz men,
> Vil Inglande nivr si agen;

> Obit 24, Kal. Dekembris, 1247
>
> Christmas Eve

Robin Hood's Bay in the parish of Fylingdale, six miles SE of Whitby, is a small fishing town, formerly noted for being the retreat of that famous captain and his banditti; who, when closely pursued, had always in readiness at this place, a number of small fishing vessels, in which putting off to sea, he eluded the vigilance of his pursuers, and bid defiance to the whole power of the English nation, civil and military.

Christmas Changes in Sheffield

'Forget your old impressions of Sheffield – they are out of date.' So says the Sheffield Corporation's attractive brochure. 'Modern Sheffield combines the skills and traditions of the past with all the excitement of dramatic architecture, new environment, new prestige. Sheffield, changing fast, is very much a city on the move . . . That is what modern Sheffield is all about.'

So let's look at Christmas, the time when home, family and people mean most. Take carols and music first. In Sheffield Cathedral they flock to hear the Festival of Nine Lessons and Carols, and everyone turns out to hear the *Messiah* – not just to hear it, but to take part in it, for 'Messiah For All' is catching on fast.

Tha' thinks ahve been in a pub suppin' ale,
But tha'll alter thi mind when I tell thi mi tale.

Ah've bin to t'chappil to harken to t'choir.
They've bin givin' selections from Handel's *Messiah*.

There are more books and articles and newspaper reports written about carols than almost any other subject in Sheffield. It has become almost a religion, with the *Sheffield Star*'s Carols Supplement as its bible, written by Dr Ian Russell, who has also written a treatise on the subject.

The new tradition flourishes in pubs, clubs, halls and houses in a large area around Sheffield. These 'gatherings' take place anywhere, any time. For instance, the Royal Hotel at Dungworth and the Blue Ball at Worrall have carols every Sunday lunchtime between Remembrance Day and Christmas. Bands, too, like the Stammington Brass Band, play daily in the run up to Christmas. What started earlier in the century as groups of farmers and churchmen singing in harmony – all men, of course – has become folk singing on a grand scale, men and women, with 'figgy pudding,' and 'On Ilkla Moor bar t'hat' to the tune of *Cranbrook*. Not Christmas carols –

Low Shiregreen Festival

Christmas folk songs, reverting once again to the pagan origins from which most Christmas customs come.

But there are still links with the Church. You might hear resident musician David Smith at the Three Merry Lads, Lodge Moor, on Saturday nights, and then find him playing the organ at Stephen Hill Methodist Church on Sunday.

If we take one step back in time, this link between church and people was much stronger. John Shaw recalls the close harmony that existed between the churches of all denominations and the people in the twenties and thirties, remembering the parties, and the mummers with their Christmas plays taken on to the streets.

The young ones went "mummering" – small parties dressed themselves up in all types of traditional costumes, blacked their faces and went round selected houses wishing them "Merry Christmas", singing carols and enacting short plays. A typical one was "The Derby Trip". Ditties were sung, such as:

> A pocket full of money and a cellar full of beer;
> A horse and a gig and a big fat pig to last you
> all next year.

> Hole in my stocking, hole in my shoe.
> Please can you spare a copper or two?
> If you haven't any pennies, ha'penny will do,
> If you haven't any ha'pennies, God Bless You!

Many unemployed men and youths formed Jazzy Bands. The instruments – trumpets, zazaphones, dullimoes and drums – were made from scrap metal and wood and pig's bladder. Other instruments included penny whistles, nickernacks (made from beef rib bones), mouth organs and Jew's harps. They were all in fancy dress, and the proceeds went to relieve those needier than themselves.

· *A Yorkshire Christmas* ·

John Shaw also recalls the displays created by the shops at Christmas – huge tableaux of Christmas scenes. He regrets that not all progress has been for the better, though. 'One of my most lasting memories is the respect for children, women and property we all had, and the very small amount of mugging, rape, child abuse, which occurred among the poorer classes. It was virtually unknown for people to lock their doors at any time. Also there was an unwritten code, "Pay for your own china and never make a midden in your own back yard!"' And he reminds us of the tradition, 'Always mix and beat Yorkshire pudding batter on your doorstep.'

Another Sheffield resident, Harry Ferrar, takes us back further to the early years of the century when times were hard.

Ther wer no decorations in town, or Father Christmases, or owt like that in 1910. Sunday School parties, yes. No presents, just an apple or orange, that wer all.

We made kissing bows decorated wi' coloured tissue paper and sugared pigs, and papers with mottoes like 'Ours is a nice 'ouse ours is', an' a' like that. These wooden bows were taken off a butter barrel — butter wer in big barrels in them days — and two hoops put through each other made a kissing bow. Relations used to come at Christmas, to each other's houses, to see the kissing bows. No Christmas cards, and Christmas turkey wer only for the posh. We had pork, taters and veg. Mother used to make the Christmas puddings in August and keep them wrapped up in a rag. A week afore Christmas she'd make mince pies, Christmas cake and lemon curd. Ther wer football matches on Christmas Day and Boxing Day — league matches at Bram'l. We hadn't much money but all wer int' same boat. Wages were 29/6d on the trams. We stayed at home and had a good sing — Good King Wenceslas an' that.

Int' First World War all were in darkness for fear of the

115

zeppelins. We'd go carol singing tho' – went up Sunny Bank – we all got a penny given. No, ther were no bands except on Saturday neet reg'lar – the Salvation Army. That's the day we did errands for the Jews. My dad used to sell 'em chickens. We took the live chickens first to the Rabbi to be slaughtered.

Lived in Lawson Street – all back-to-backs. The yards. The 'pig yards' 'twer called. Seven yards all round the pig yard and a couple of shops. Mi Dad nivver had a day off – worked for his'sen. But we as kids laked about an' a' like that. It wer different then.

Boxing Day Cricket and Football

My first Christmas in Leeds also marked my introduction to Yorkshire cricket, rubbing shoulders with the famous – Brian Close, Hutton (was it Len or Richard, or both?), Ray Illingworth – the names too numerous to remember. All this on a cold, frosty Boxing Day. It didn't matter who was playing whom or what the score was. The weather mattered, though. Too much snow and it was off, but crisp, white and frosty was the perfect setting for cricket, sustained by mulled wine and hot grog to wash down the pork pie and sausage rolls. This was a foretaste of summer.

The old rivalry of the Roses between Lancashire and Yorkshire is never better demonstrated than when the North of England's own 'test matches' are played at Old Trafford or Headingley. How inscrutable the expressions on the faces as you scan the ring round the pitch. Picnics galore – flasks, sandwiches, beer cans, buckets of tea. The men's heads covered with knotted handkerchiefs; businessmen in shirt sleeves muttering advice to their team – 'Get on with it.'

The tradition is to talk in a loud enough voice for everyone around you to hear – including any player on the field if you've a message for him. But woe betide the intruder in these affairs.

A southern spectator at a Roses game once applauded a fine stroke by the batsman.

'Well played!' he called out.

The stocky fellow on his right turned to him and asked, 'Dosta belong to Lancashire?'

'No,' replied the visitor.

His neighbour on the left joined in with, 'Dosta come fra' Yorkshire then?'

'No,' he said.

Both men looked at him and said together, 'Well, mind thi' own bloody business then!'

One of Scarborough's most popular Boxing Day customs is the Fishermen's and Firemen's charity football match on the south sands. It originated 96 years ago from the loss at sea of a local fishing smack.

On Saturday 18 November 1893, a violent storm hit the north-east coast, causing havoc on land and wrecking many vessels in the North Sea. Scarborough was battered by a hurricane for three days, and three ships were wrecked in the South Bay. When the storm struck there were twenty Scarborough smacks at sea, most of them in Scottish waters, and all but one returned home. The missing one was a 55-ton smack called *Evelyn and Maud*, built at Scarborough in 1873.

On 2 December, wreckage and a lifebelt from the *Evelyn and Maud* was washed up at Easington, near the mouth of the Humber, and a piece of bone was found there on which was written 'Ship Going Down. Sinking Fast. *Evelyn and Maud.*' One woman was able to identify the writing as her husband's, and it was finally accepted that the smack and all its crew had perished at sea.

The owner and the Mayor launched a public fund to support the bereaved families – five widows and nine dependent children. Three local fishermen organized a football match in aid of the fund, and the teams were drawn from fishermen and stokers of Scarborough's steam-trawler fleet. On Christmas Day morning the match took place at the Ebor Football Ground, and the firemen won 4–1. There were 1,500 spectators, and they contributed about £9 to a collection!

The Christmas Day match was so popular that it became an annual event, and in 1897 a tug-of-war was also held. In 1898

Christmas advertisements, 1927 and 1949

the football match and the tug-of-war were held on Boxing Day on the south sands – the fishermen winning the football match and the firemen the tug-of-war – and £40 was collected from the large crowd. Thereafter the events continued annually on Boxing Day on the south sands, and much money was raised for local charities.

In 1901 a comic aspect was introduced, with grotesque characters providing entertainment, collectors and supporters wearing costumes, and local bands playing – the best-known being the Buffs Comic Band. The teams wore top hats – white for fishermen and red for firemen – and in 1904 they sported coloured shirts to match.

The Fishermen's and Firemen's Charity, officially founded in 1904, still organizes the Boxing Day football match, and the money collected goes to provide vouchers for pensioners, the sick and the disabled who are connected in some way with the fishing community of Scarborough.

It Was Night

EMILY BRONTË

It was night, and on the mountains
Fathoms deep the snow-drifts lay;
Streams and waterfalls and fountains
Down in darkness stole away.

Long ago the hopeless peasant
Left his sheep all buried there:
Sheep that through the summer pleasant
He had watched with fondest care.

Now no more a cheerful ranger
Following pathways known of yore,
Sad he stood a wildered stranger
On his own unbounded moor.

The Diaries of Anne Lister

Anne Lister (1791–1840) was an unconventional upper-class woman who lived in Halifax and Shibden Hall, West Yorkshire. An intrepid traveller, she died in the Caucasian mountains. Her prodigious diaries are held in the archives of Calderdale Museum.

Halifax, Thursday, 25th December 1817

We all went to morning church and stayed the sacrament. Assisted my aunt in reading prayers in the afternoon. In the evening, read aloud sermons 8 and 9, Hoole. A remarkably fine, frosty day. Roads very slippery. Barometer $1\frac{1}{2}$ deg. above changeable. Fahr. 29° at 9 p.m.

· *A Yorkshire Christmas* ·

Halifax, Friday, 26th December 1817

Went without dinner today, not having felt well since I came home (bilious and heavy) which I solely attribute to dining at 3 p.m. and which certainly never agrees with me. Went downstairs to dessert and then walked to meet 'M' on her way from York to Lawton, through Leeds by Burstall, and met her (and the cook, Elizabeth, she had hired in York) in the landau a few yards beyond the Hipperholme bar. I was pleased to find she had very good horses and very civil drivers from the Rose & Crown (Leeds) and which were in readiness according to my orders at one, exactly the time she reached Leeds. 'M' arrived here at five by the kitchen clock, three-quarters past four by the Halifax, and quarter-past four by Leeds and York. She brought me a small parcel from Nantz, containing a very kind note from herself and one from Lou, and a pair of cambric

Head office, Halifax Building Society, 1957 – Christmas?

muslin sleeves with broad wrist bands to be worn as linings, which she (Nantz) had made, and another pair which she had altered for me. After tea, 'M' and I played whist against my uncle and aunt and won a rubber of four and a game. Very fine, frosty day.

Came upstairs twenty minutes before eleven, but sat up talking till twelve. After all, I believe 'M's' heart is all my own. 'M' told us, after tea, what a narrow escape Mr C—— L—— had just had the other day of being shot. In getting over a hedge, something caught the trigger, the gun went off and the contents only just missed. A similar accident, I understand, occurred to him just before 'M' and Louisa left Lawton, and his glove and waistcoat were a good deal burnt.

Halifax, 25th December 1818

We all walked to morning church. Mr West of Southowram preached. Afterwards wished us 'A merry Christmas'. All stayed the sacrament. I fear I never received it with less feeling of reverence. Was thinking more of Miss Browne than anything else. She was there opposite me at the altar table.

Halifax, 26th December 1818

Went down the north parade and sat half an hour at Cross-hills. The whole kit of them at home and vulgar as ever. Miss Caroline's head like a porcupine. Surely Mrs Greenwood must drink . . . During supper, fired the pistols.

Halifax, 28th December 1818

My aunt and I set off to Halifax at half-past two, she having, just before, gathered out of the garden for my Aunt Lister, a nosegay of fifteen different sorts of flowers – laurustinus,

chrysanthemums, yellow jasmine, pink-tree flower, dwarf passion-flower, heart's ease, double primrose, purple stock, auricula, sweet allison, Venus's looking-glass, gentianella, roses, larkspur, and pheasant's eye – and three or four more sorts might have been added, such has been this uncommon season.

Halifax, Friday, 31st December 1819

In the afternoon . . . to the Saltmarshes'. Stayed rather above an hour and got home at 5.10. Better satisfied with my visit than usual. Thought them glad enough to see me and I said nothing I wished unsaid. From Emma's account, their ball must have been a riotous concern. The Greenwoods and Miss Mary Haigue danced riotously and Tom Rawson took Mrs Prescott and danced her on his knee before them all, having before as publicly tickled her daughter, Elizabeth, on the sofa. She and Miss Mary Haigue afterwards went into another room. Tom kissed them both. Emma was obliged to leave them and Mr Saltmarshe and Mrs Walker of Crow Nest unluckily went in together and caught them. He had his arm round Mary Haigue's neck, but she looked nothing abashed. Mrs Christopher Rawson took Miss Astley with her, the Unitarian Minister's sister. Tom said, 'It is a long time since I have had a kiss of you.' Mr Christopher gave her one, said the ladies will think it rude if it does not go round, and though he had never seen Miss Astley before, put his arm round her neck and kissed her also.

A good deal of snow fell last night and the morning was snowy till after ten.

Friday, 21st December 1821, at York

The mare stiffish and rather knocked up with her journey yesterday, and I could not get off from Low Grange till eleven.

123

Drove off in the midst of wind and rain which were just come on. Tried the mare with a pint of warm ale at Simpson's but she would not touch, nor did she eat well this morning or yesterday. Never saw an animal so idle and sluggish withal. She took more whipping even than yesterday and, a little beyond Barby Moor new inn, seemed determined to go no further. Went back to the house to get a poster. The man at the inn said it would break a pair. His horses were much worked by the coaches, etc., and civilly but positively said he really could not let me have a horse. Gave the mare a little warm water and made George drive forwards to York. The mare stopped two or three times and would turn in at two or three public houses by the way, and by dint of hard whipping brought us here at last (Dr Belcombe's, Petergate) in four hours . . . So sleepy with being so much out in the air, and so harassed one way or other that I could scarce keep my eyes open and was obliged to come upstairs to bed directly after tea.

Sunday, 25th December 1821, at York

'M' and I went to speak to Mrs Small in College Street, who keeps the most respectable register office for servants in York. We then went to the Minster in time for the anthem, and walked about the aisles till service was over. What a magnificent building. How striking the effect of its being lighted up throughout! Which it is every Sunday, and was today . . .

After dinner, all danced and made merry with the children, and I, while they played with them, came upstairs and finished the journal of yesterday and wrote this of today.

Winter Storms

EMILY BRONTË

Wild the road and rough and dreary;
Barren all the moorland round;
Rude the couch that rests us weary;
Mossy stone and heathy ground.

But, when winter storms were meeting
In the moonless, midnight dome,
Did we heed the tempest's beating,
Howling round our spirits' home?

No; that tree with branches riven,
Whitening in the whirl of snow,
As it tossed against the heaven,
Sheltered happy hearts below —

Christmas Cake and Cheese

The first Christmas I spent in Yorkshire was in 1950, and one memory left of that festive occasion is 'Christmas cake and cheese'. As a Londoner, I had never met it before, but now, a Northerner by choice, I never eat Christmas cake without *real* cheese.

Wensleydale is the premier cheese of England, and we have the monks of Rievaulx Abbey in 1150 to thank for it. Rievaulx Abbey in the middle of the twelfth century, when the famous Ailred was its third Abbot, had a complement of 140 monks and 500 lay brothers 'so that the church swarmed with them, like a hive with bees'. Even nowadays that would be a surprisingly large population for this quiet valley; then it must have created a considerable demand for agricultural products in addition to what the lay brothers could provide themselves, and a great deal of employment besides.

Large quantities of cheese (which used to be made from ewes' milk) were consumed at Bolton Abbey and Jervaulx Abbey. Wensleydale cheese is now a factory product, but when it was first made in those days much of it was produced by women outside the monasteries, as were many other essential commodities.

The term Wensleydale became the generic name for the cheese in 1840 when cheese fairs were first held at Leyburn. It is a white cheese made from a finely-cut curd, lightly pressed to retain a high moisture content. This makes the cheese

slightly crumbly and flaky. Dales folk have not been satisfied in recent years with the quality of their locally-produced Wensleydale, because most of it is 'dairy made'.

All the same, some of the farmhouse techniques were quite crude. They used pieces of men's old shirts for bandaging, and calico had to be insisted on. Curds were crudely tried for acidity by testing with a red-hot poker held an inch off. Cheese had to be firm but not too firm. Many farmers' wives made good cheese, but some was too soft, or tasted of onion where the cows had eaten garlic. It was a common sight to see crudely painted signs offering 'Home-made Wensleydale' to motorists.

However, the signs are reappearing. In Swaledale, for instance, a super semi-soft cheese from Jersey cows is on offer, and near Ripon the Fountains Dairy has revived Coverdale alongside its Wensleydale. In Bedale you can now get sheep's-milk cheese called Jorvik, and a new cheese called Jervaulx. In the Ribble valley there is a red Windsor containing elderberry wine and a cheese called 'Yorkshire's Own'.

All that is fine, and you can try them all over Christmas, but there is only one cheese to eat with Christmas cake – moist, flaky, delicate – Wensleydale. It may be a pale shadow of its former self, but it lives on as 'one of the world's classic cheeses'.

And here's a recipe for a Rich Christmas Cake to go with it, published in Leeds in 1909.

11 oz butter	$\frac{1}{4}$ lb blanched almonds, sliced
11 oz flour	$\frac{1}{2}$ lb candied peel
10 oz castor sugar	1 wineglassful brandy
1 lb raisins	6 eggs
1 lb currants, chopped	$\frac{1}{2}$ oz mixed spice

Beat the butter to a cream, add the sugar, then the eggs well beaten alternately with the flour, beat well and add the

remainder of the ingredients in small quantities. When well mixed turn onto a tin lined with paper and bake in a moderate oven $3\frac{1}{2}$ to 4 hours.

The mixture rises very little, so the cake should be made nearly as deep as you want it to be.

Yorkshire

'Yorkshire' was the title given to this popular Christmas hymn-tune written by John Wainwright (1723–1786), a well-known church organist and composer, in 1750. The words were written by John Byrom (1692–1763).

· A Yorkshire Christmas ·

Christians, awake, salute the happy morn,
Whereon the Saviour of the world was born;
Rise to adore the mystery of love,
Which hosts of Angels chanted from above;
With them the joyful tidings first begun
Of God incarnate and the Virgin's Son:

Then to the watchful shepherds it was told,
Who heard the angelic herald's voice, 'Behold,
I bring good tidings of a Saviour's birth
To you and all the nations upon earth;
This day hath God fulfilled his promised word,
This day is born a Saviour, Christ the Lord.'

A Christmas Broadcast

WILLIAM TEMPLE

William Temple was Archbishop of York from 1929–42 before becoming Archbishop of Canterbury. His untimely death in 1944 brought a remarkable career to an end. Well known for addressing the issues of unemployment and homelessness, the Prime Minister of the day, Chamberlain, said of him: 'I wish the Archbishop of York would mind his own business.' Temple's response was, 'To the man who is better off, I suggest he should say, "If there is not enough for both of us to get something, please give it to him".'

All kinds of people, whatever their religious beliefs or disbeliefs, have adopted Christmas as the festival of family and friendship. It is a great thing to have such a festival generally recognized, whether its religious basis is accepted or not. It helps to keep together friendships which may be drifting into forgetfulness, and it strengthens the bonds of affection alike between friends and among kinsfolk. Christmas is itself a very real influence for the maintenance of goodwill amongst men.

But it has only come to have that character because of what Christian people have regarded as its true significance for all the centuries since men first observed it. What Christians commemorate today is not merely the Birth of a Child who

grew up to be a remarkable man; it is the turning point of human history and the appearance within it of the Eternal God revealing Himself in a human life. 'The Word was made flesh, and we beheld His glory.'

As the generations pass, men's knowledge increases and their habits of thought change. The framework in which they set that central figure varies almost indefinitely from age to age; but the Figure itself remains, and always again makes good the claim to the central place in the thought and the loyalty of men . . .

We clamour to know the character of Ultimate Reality; the Gospel points us to Jesus Christ. 'Lord, show us the Father and it sufficeth us. "He that hath seen Me hath seen the Father."'

> I say, the acknowledgement of God in Christ
> Accepted by thy reason, solves for thee
> All questions in the world and out of it,
> And has so far advanced thee to be wise.

It is this which gives to Christmas its significance. And here I want to insist that the value of this belief depends primarily upon its truth. If it is a beautiful fiction, its power is gone. The claim of the Christian Gospel is not chiefly that it is uplifting, or that it is comforting, or that it meets our needs, or that it cures our spiritual diseases. Its claim is first and foremost that it is true. If it is true, all those other benefits follow; but if it is not true, they do not follow.

Moreover this truth is to be grasped in all its glorious and overwhelming paradox. That paradox is at its height on Christmas Day. When we think of God in Christ upon the Cross, we are thinking of Him as revealed in One whose love never failed before the worst attacks and insults of malice and contempt. When we think of God in Christ risen from the dead, we are thinking of Him as revealed in One who

overcame the last enemy of man. On Good Friday or Easter Day the characteristic of Christ to which our minds are turned is one which we readily conceive to be an attribute of Divine Majesty. But today we are called to worship the Baby in the manger. Here is the most awe-inspiring mystery of all:

That the great Angell-blincking light should shrinke
His blaze, to shine in a poore shepherd's eye;
That the unmeasur'd God so low should sinke
As Pris'ner in a few poore Rags to lye;
That from His Mother's Brest he milke should drinke
Who feeds with Nectar Heav'n's faire family;
   That a vile Manger His low Bed should prove,
   Who in a Throne of stars Thunders above.

So let us feast and be merry, not because tomorrow we die but because today Jesus Christ is born; and if that is the reason for our merriment, it will be such as to bring no sorrow in its train. If we Christian folk believed our own Gospel wholeheartedly and lived in any degree worthily of it, we should be full of an infectious gaiety. Our faith is feeble, and our lives do not correspond with it. There must be in our religion other factors besides joy and mirth. But today when heaven and earth unite; when angels couple together God's glory and man's peace; when Love comes down — Love all lovely, all divine — to make its home on earth; today let us be merry in the presence of God. And when today is over let us carry that divine merriment into our sombre and busy lives, and let all our mirth be such as Love Divine inspires.

So it will be with us if we can join the Shepherds and the Kings in their worship at the manger cradle. For to worship is to humble one's self before Him to whom worship is given and open one's heart to receive Him. If we can humble ourselves before the innocence of helpless childhood and open our hearts

to receive its simplicity, its trustfulness, its happiness, its love, then for us too Christmas will have been the birthday of Love Divine in the hearts to which we invite and welcome Him. Once more then, as when the day began, so now as it draws to a close – Come let us adore Him, Christ the Lord.

Christmas Day, 1066 AD

On this historic day, the invader William, Duke of Normandy, was crowned King of England in Westminster Abbey by Archbishop Aldred of York. Events leading up to this began a year earlier, on 5 January 1066, when Edward the Confessor died. The following day, Harold, second son of Godwin, Earl of Kent, was elected King.

The new King was faced by two imminent invasions, one from the united fleets of Tostig and Hardrada, 300 ships strong, waiting off the Scottish coast, the other from Duke William of Normandy, whose fleet of 800 ships was assembled across the Channel. England's future then, as on later occasions, depended on the sea. A wind from the north would bring the Norsemen and prevent William's fleet from sailing. A wind from the south would help the Normans and hold back the waiting fleet off Scotland.

The north wind blew first, and with it the fleets of

Norsemen sailed down the coast, attacking and burning Scarborough on the way, and into the Humber. Harold acted quickly, marching north to York, and found the invaders camped seven miles away on the Derwent at Stamford Bridge. Within the day, Hardrada and Tostig were dead, their troops slaughtered or in retreat. Of the 300 ships which had sailed into the Humber only twenty-four returned.

Three days later Duke William's army landed near Hastings. The change of wind which had helped William kept Harold's fleet bottled up in the Thames. There was no alternative but for him to make a forced march back to the south with the army that had defeated the Norsemen. The journey from York to London was accomplished in five days, and four days later his army was on its way to the heights above Hastings to meet the new threat. The story of the battle has been told many times and is pictured in the Bayeux Tapestry. Once again fate played its part. The twist of fortune that killed Harold by a Norman arrow, rather than William by a Saxon axe, decided the fate of England.

Coaches and Christmas Cards

The speed and romance of coaching attracted the young aristocracy and gentry. The crack of the whip, the sound of the

horn and the drumming of the hooves and a glamour that disappeared more suddenly than we can imagine when the railways came.

But the Victorians' nostalgia for the coach lingers on today, in a thousand Christmas cards, and is immortalized in Dickens' Christmas novels.

Coaching brought prosperity to Yorkshire, where thousands were employed in the industry, providing horses, carriages, inns, food and all the trappings of travel and tourism. Even peers of the realm took the reins, as they do today, but we have lost the drama of the dawn departure, the coaching inns, the broken axles and the dangers of ice and snow.

York has a very special claim to fame, in that it was here at No. 114 Micklegate that Joseph Hansom was born. Joseph was a designer, not only of the famous Hansom Cab (one can be seen in the Castle Museum at York), but also of churches, the most renowned being Arundel Cathedral. Micklegate was then the main thoroughfare, paved with stone setts to assist the horses' grip on the steep incline. Even in the days of the horse-tram, it needed an extra horse to be harnessed to pull the tram up the hill at its steepest part.

The largest Yorkshire coach operator, however, was Outhwaite of Leeds, whose network of routes nation-wide was prodigious.

Charles Dickens joined the stagecoach set for his numerous trips to York to see his brother who worked in Micklegate. It was the advent of the stagecoach which spread the practice of sending Christmas cards and presents, as it established a cheap system of distributing the Royal Mail – though not always on time.

There were dangers, too. In 1837 a young man fell from the Leeds–Manchester 'Umpire'. The coachman pulled up as soon as he could to find the lad 'lying by the hind wheel, his left leg wrenched off at the knee'. He had been clinging to the coach

for the ride. 'A very dangerous practice to which boys are much addicted.' Another young man on top of the coach then 'swooned away at the melancholy sight and fell with great force from the vehicle, the front part of his head coming in contact with the ground. The blood gushed from him profusely.'

One mail guard was thrown from the coach on another occasion and was knocked unconscious. 'As he came to, he believed there was something wrong with his head. He felt a flat surface which he was convinced in his confused state was a section of his neck, his head having been cut off.' It was, in fact, the crown of his hat which had been forced down over his face!

In the winter of 1827 the Leeds–Wakefield stagecoach, 'True Blue', was travelling down Belle Hill. No brakes, of course, were fitted, and the coachman allowed the horses to gallop out of control so that the coach began to rock and sway. William Lee, a Leeds spirit merchant travelling in the coach, called out in alarm to no avail. At the bottom of the hill, where the coachman might have regained control, he was 'paralysed' with 'self-possession'. When he was aroused, he flogged the horses, and hit a number of carts parked in the road. The coach wheel locked and the coach turned over, 'horses' feet and wheels striking fire like lightning in the darkness'. James Burrell, a Knaresborough passenger, was crying out with the weight of the coach on his thigh. His leg was amputated, but he died during the night. Charles Cope, a Leeds artist, was also killed.

There was danger from mechanical and human failure, and not least from the horses, whose natural reaction to danger was to run as fast as possible away from the scene. There was a great demand for that fine breed of horse, the Cleveland from North Yorkshire – short-legged, quick-stepping horses specially bred for coach work.

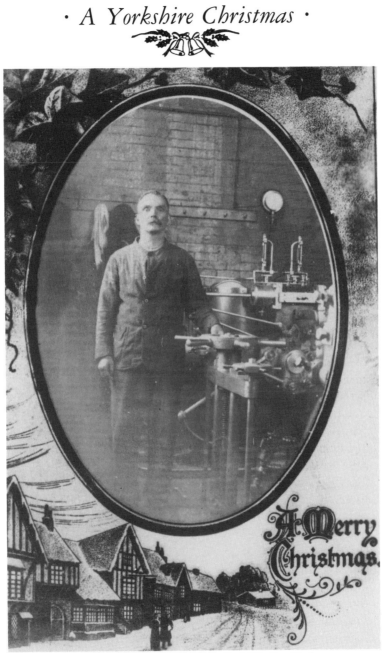

Christmas card from Drummond's Mill, Bradford

· A Yorkshire Christmas ·

It was in Cleveland, too, that the first coaches on rails were run. George Stephenson, the great railway pioneer, built the line from Pickering to Whitby to replace the stagecoaches and packhorses that also worked the route. In 1832 he reported that his scheme would 'afford the inhabitants of Whitby an increased activity of trade, the landowners an opportunity of converting an immense tract of barren soil into fertile land, and the inhabitants of Pickering cheaper and better quality coal and other commodities from Whitby'. At immense cost (£105,600) and with great difficulty the line was built across bogs and rivers and through tunnels – but the climb to Newton Dale lay ahead. It was 1,500 yards long with a gradient of 1 in 15. The first train ran in 1836, leaving Whitby to the sound of church bells, and was greeted in Pickering by cannon fire. The two original coaches, 'Hilda' and 'Premier', were in fact conventional stage coaches mounted on wheels to fit the track. The driver sat up front on the dickey, urging on the horses and operating a brake lever. The horses were used in stages, and on downward stretches they were taken off so that the coaches free-wheeled, sometimes at speeds of up to 30 mph, and this 'gratified those who delight in quickly passing thro' the air'. But at the top of Newton Dale the coaches had to be hauled up by rope. At the Bank Top there was a 10 ft diameter revolving drum with a rope wound round it, one end attached to a water tank on wheels. The tank was filled up until it outweighed the coaches. Down the far side went the water tank; up came the coaches. 'A quaint way to run a railway,' remarked Charles Dickens, or words to that effect!

Traditional Christmas festivities and weather brought their own special problems for coaches and drivers. 'No matter how good the horses, if the coachman was drunk there would be trouble.' William Bramley, who drove the 'Rockingham' north of Leeds, was always more or less drunk.

· A Yorkshire Christmas ·

In 1838 the 'York Mail' went over Blackstone Edge, and when passing over the fells crews had to be strapped to their seats. One enterprising coachman, Moses Nobbs, once had his coach blown over and thereafter, whenever the wind blew a gale, 'he took the precaution of opening both doors and tying them back, so that the wind might pass through them'. Hard luck on the passengers!

Winter brought fog, ice and snow, and in the icy conditions horses were prone to fall. In deepest winter passengers would arrive at York unable to move and have to be helped down and placed on straw in front of the fire to thaw out. It is recorded in *The Times*, 23 January 1823, that Thomas Turner, coachman of the 'Halifax and Pontefract Mail', was 'so much frozen during the late frost as to render it necessary to procure assistance to lift him from his box seat on his arrival at the Griffin Inn, Halifax'. A bottle of 'Old Scotch' was kept specially for the purpose of completing the cure. 'But the effect on me for some weeks was anything but pleasant,' one sufferer recalled.

Snow on Saturday, Chrismas Eve 1836, was worse than it had been within living memory and continued all over Christmas. North winds created blizzard conditions, 'huge drifts were formed, many like enormous wreaths, and as soon as passages were cut through, snow was driven back choking up the roads again.' London was impossible to reach from the North and the whole network was in chaos. Stables were completely exhausted of horses owing to the non-arrival of beasts from the country. On the road the horses were reported in *The Times* as being 'dead beat' from struggling through the snow, 'sobbing and sweating'. Moses Nobbs was clearly a survivor. He 'rode and tramped through terrible weather for 50 hours without a break seeing the mail through'.

But let's finish with one of those Christmas anecdotes from *The Times*, dated 26 December 1822: The 'York Mail' guard

had the surprise of his life when he started unloading the mail at the Cross Keys, Hull, at 6 o'clock on a freezing December morning just before Christmas. He discovered a chicken roosting on top of the coach. It had apparently travelled all the way from York undisturbed by the motion!

Christmas Folklore

Christmas customs, the blazing yule log, belly-filling feasts, and evergreens, mark the winter solstice on 21 December, when the sun begins to climb in the sky, the days lengthen and the earth stirs at the thought of spring and another year.

From his Yorkshire home, in 1898, Richard Blakeborough wrote:

Our greatest observance of custom is, as it should be, in connexion with Christmas-tide; indeed, preparation for the

same really commences some weeks in advance. There is the pudding to make and partly boil; all ingredients for the plum-cake to order; the mincemeat to prepare for the mince-pies; the goose to choose from some neighbouring farmer's stock; the cheese to buy; and the wheat to have hullins beaten off and to cree, for the all important frumenty; the yule-cake or pepper-cake to make; the hollin to gather . . .

A wheat sheaf of gleaned corn was hung from the kitchen rafters to be used in making the Christmas 'frumenty'. So much the better if the wheat could be gleaned from one of the Abbeys at Fountains or Rievaulx. Once eaten, no more was to be made until the following year. The yule-cakes, made of flour, yeast, raisins, currants, lemon peel and nutmeg, were over twelve inches in diameter and three inches thick, criss-crossed with pastry strips. They were washed down with a glass of Yorkshire mulled ale or elderberry wine and a slice of Wensleydale cheese on which a cross was engraved – and no doubt a good dose of milk of magnesia!

Yorkshire's 'twelve days of madness' were full of bewitching folklore. The dairy was a natural source of stories of fairies and witches, who turned the milk or kept it fresh, who made the butter set or not, as the case may be. And hush! At midnight the cattle in the byre knelt and wept, then spoke if you were there to witness it. The Yorkshire pudding which you ate with your goose or turkey must be made with the first rich milk – thick and yellow – taken from a cow after calving. And the jug had to be returned to the dairy unwashed to bring good luck on the herd and on the village.

The puddings, jams and sauces must all be stirred sun-wise to appease the sun god, and bread must not be burnt on the fire or thrown away. Black pudding must be dedicated to a person. Christmas, not New Year, was 'let in' by a dark-haired

· A Yorkshire Christmas ·

man entering with a sprig of greenery to collect a penny from the hearth. 'No persons (boys excepted) ever presumed to go out of doors till the threshold had been consecrated by the entrance of a male. Females had no part in this matter, and if a damsel, lovely as an angel, entered first, her fair form was viewed with horror as an image of death.'

But evil spirits were about. They turned the milk, turned the head and brought bad luck to the home, the cattle and the fields. As one old lady explained, 'No, I doan say as I believe in witches, but certainly i' former times there were wizards and buzzards and them sort of things. No, I doan say 'at ther' are now, but I do believe in a yevil eye.'

Amulets of holed stones like a heavy necklace were hung with loops of rowan over doors and on barns to ward off the

evil spirits, and at Christmas, wheeling a horse thrice before a door was believed to be particularly efficacious.

The unluckiest day of all was Childermas, or Holy Innocents' Day, on 28 December, commemorating the slaughter of the children by King Herod in the Holy Land. No washing was to be hung out on that day or it would be covered in blood, church bells were muffled, and if a child happened to be born, ill health would follow. All silly and fanciful? I can only say that my own father was born on Childermas, and he caught pneumonia which never left him, so that he died soon after his forty-seventh birthday.

Wassailers did their best to bring good luck. The word comes from 'was hail' or 'be fortunate'. The wassailers marched through the village during the twelve days of celebration, holding great wooden bowls with iron heads, decorated with ribbons and evergreens and filled with hot ale, roasted crab-apples, toast, nutmeg, sugar and eggs. Offering their steaming, sweet-smelling bowls to the villagers, they sang:

> Wassail! Wassail! All over the town,
> Our toast is white, our ale is brown,
> Our bowl is made of the maple tree,
> We be good fellows, I drink to thee.

Yorkshire wassailers also carried boxes with images of the Virgin Mary, the Holy Child and the three wise men or kings, set amid evergreens, with tinsel, spice and an orange representing the three gifts. These were referred to as the 'Advent Images' and a donation was rewarded with a piece of greenery from the boxes for good luck – and as a sure and certain cure for toothache! To be missed by the wassailers was regarded as unlucky, hence that nineteenth-century Yorkshire saying, 'As unhappy as a man who has seen no Advent Images.' In Leeds the box was called a 'milly box' (a corruption of 'My Lady's Box').

Associated with this custom was another, the 'Brumble' or Christmas Eve party, the centrepiece of which was the Wassail Bowl. The bowl was filled with 'Lambswool', a brew consisting of apples, strong ale, cinnamon, ginger, nutmeg, cloves and rum or brandy. The main dish was Hot Pot and pickles, and the chief entertainment a game of whist, followed by dancing to a band – pretty strenuous it was, too. Guests entertained each other, and 'if anybody hung back and wouldna sing nor prate nor even dance when called upon, everybody shouted "earn your keep, earn your keep," and the bashful one was minded of the good things he had put away, and the drinks that had cooled his throat, and in return for hospitality would do the best he could.' And woe betide the card-player who revoked or who forgot trumps!

According to folklore, there used to be a custom of 'watching with the bees', whereby watchers of the beehives at midnight were supposed to determine the exact time of Jesus' birth by a loud, incessant humming of the bees. In other places it was customary to toll the church bell as for the dead to show that the Christ-child had killed the hatred in the world and the spite of the Devil. At a church in Dewsbury they ring the 'Devil's Knell' – one stroke for every year since Christ's birth.

A sheaf of corn was hung over the doorway of the church so that birds from the riverside willows and frozen fields could participate in the feast. There was the usual Christmas morning service in church, when the congregation would stand up and chant, 'Ule, Ule, Ule' to rejoice at the coming of the Lord. Outside, they would sing:

> Ule! Ule! Ule! Ule!
> Three puddings in a pule,
> Crack nuts and cry Ule!

· A Yorkshire Christmas ·

In the North Riding it was the custom, after receiving the Sacrament on Christmas Day, 'to go from church directly to the ale-house and there drink together as a testimony of charity and friendship'.

Nowadays, driving across the winter-black, mist-enshrouded moors, the inevitable wind roaming through the villages brings strange and unsettling sounds. On such nights the local inn becomes the centre of activity and gossip, and the reciting of oral traditions. When poet Philip Larkin, whom I met in Cottingham, was asked why he chose to live in Hull, he replied, 'It was one of the most difficult places I knew to travel to.' But change has come and, as the innkeeper said, 'There's nowt so permanent as change.'

from

Jane Eyre

CHARLOTTE BRONTË

The ground was hard, the air was still, my road was lonely; I walked fast till I got warm, and then I walked slowly to enjoy and analyse the species of pleasure brooding for me in the hour and situation. It was three o'clock; the church bell tolled as I passed under the belfry: the charm of the hour lay in its approaching dimness, in the low-gliding and pale-beaming sun. I was a mile from Thornfield, in a lane noted for wild roses in summer, for nuts and blackberries in autumn, and even now possessing a few coral treasures in hips and haws, but whose best winter delight lay in its utter solitude and leafless repose. If a breath of air stirred, it made no sound here; for there was not a holly, not an evergreen to rustle, and the stripped hawthorn and hazel bushes were as still as the white, worn stones which causewayed the middle of the path. Far and wide, on each side, there were only fields, where no cattle now browsed; and the little brown birds, which stirred occasionally in the hedge, looked like single russet leaves that had forgotten to drop.

This lane inclined up-hill all the way to Hay; having reached the middle, I sat down on a stile which led thence into a field. Gathering my mantle about me, and sheltering my hands in my muff, I did not feel the cold, though it froze

keenly; as was attested by a sheet of ice covering the causeway, where a little brooklet, now congealed, had overflowed after a rapid thaw some days since. From my seat I could look down on Thornfield: the grey and battlemented hall was the principal object in the vale below me; its woods and dark rookery rose against the west. I lingered till the sun went down amongst the trees, and sank crimson and clear behind them. I then turned eastward.

On the hill-top above me sat the rising moon; pale yet as a cloud, but brightening momentarily, she looked over Hay, which, half lost in trees, sent up a blue smoke from its few chimneys: it was yet a mile distant, but in the absolute hush I could hear plainly its thin murmurs of life. My ear, too, felt the flow of currents; in what dales and depths I could not tell: but there were many hills beyond Hay, and doubtless many becks threading their passes. That evening calm betrayed alike the tinkle of the nearest streams, the sough of the most remote.

A rude noise broke on these fine ripplings and whisperings, at once so far away and so clear: a positive tramp, tramp, a metallic clatter, which effaced the soft wave-wanderings; as, in a picture, the solid mass of a crag, or the rough boles of a great oak, drawn in dark and strong on the foreground, efface the aerial distance of azure hill, sunny horizon, and blended clouds where tint melts into tint.

The din was on the causeway: a horse was coming; the windings of the lane yet hid it, but it approached. I was just leaving the stile; yet, as the path was narrow, I sat still to let it go by. In those days I was young, and all sorts of fancies bright and dark tenanted my mind: the memories of nursery stories were there amongst other rubbish; and when they recurred, maturing youth added to them a vigour and vividness beyond what childhood could give. As this horse approached, and as I watched for it to appear through the dusk, I remembered

certain of Bessie's tales, wherein figured a North-of-England spirit called a 'Gytrash,' which, in the form of horse, mule, or large dog, haunted solitary ways, and sometimes came upon belated travellers, as this horse was now coming upon me.

It was very near, but not yet in sight; when, in addition to the tramp, tramp, I heard a rush under the hedge, and close down by the hazel stems glided a great dog, whose black and white colour made him a distinct object against the trees. It was exactly one form of Bessie's Gytrash – a lion-like creature with long hair and a huge head: it passed me, however, quietly enough; not staying to look up, with strange pretercanine eyes, in my face, as I half expected it would. The horse followed, – a tall steed, and on its back a rider. The man, the human being, broke the spell at once. Nothing ever rode the Gytrash: it was always alone; and goblins, to my notions, though they might tenant the dumb carcasses of beasts, could scarce covet shelter in the commonplace human form. No Gytrash was this, – only a traveller taking the short cut to Millcote. He passed, and I went on; a few steps, and I turned: a sliding sound and an exclamation of 'What the deuce is to do now?' and a clattering tumble, arrested my attention. Man and horse were down; they had slipped on the sheet of ice which glazed the causeway. The dog came bounding back, and seeing his master in a predicament, and hearing the horse groan, barked till the evening hills echoed the sound, which was deep in proportion to his magnitude. He snuffed round the prostrate group, and then he ran up to me; it was all he could do, – there was no other help at hand to summon. I obeyed him, and walked down to the traveller, by this time struggling himself free of his steed. His efforts were so vigorous, I thought he could not be much hurt; but I asked him the question –

'Are you injured, sir?'

* * *

'Is Mr Rochester gone anywhere? I did not know he was out.'

'Oh, he set off the moment he had breakfasted! He is gone to the Leas, Mr Eshton's place, ten miles on the other side Millcote. I believe there is quite a party assembled there; Lord Ingram, Sir George Lynn, Colonel Dent, and others.'

'Do you expect him back to-night?'

'No – nor to-morrow either; I should think he is very likely to stay a week or more: when these fine, fashionable people get together, they are so surrounded by elegance and gaiety, so well provided with all that can please and entertain, they are in no hurry to separate. Gentlemen especially are often in request on such occasions; and Mr Rochester is so talented and so lively in society, that I believe he is a general favourite: the ladies are very fond of him; though you would not think his appearance calculated to recommend him particularly in their eyes: but I suppose his acquirements and abilities, perhaps his wealth and good blood, make amends for any little fault of look.'

'Are there ladies at the Leas?'

'There are Mrs Eshton and her three daughters – very elegant young ladies indeed; and there are the Honourable Blanche and Mary Ingram, most beautiful women, I suppose: indeed I have seen Blanche, six or seven years since, when she was a girl of eighteen. She came here to a Christmas ball and party Mr Rochester gave. You should have seen the dining-room that day – how richly it was decorated, how brilliantly lit up! I should think there were fifty ladies and gentlemen present – all of the first county families; and Miss Ingram was considered the belle of the evening.'

'You saw her, you say, Mrs Fairfax: what was she like?'

'Yes, I saw her. The dining-room doors were thrown open; and, as it was Christmas-time, the servants were allowed to assemble in the hall, to hear some of the ladies sing and play. Mr Rochester would have me to come in, and I sat down in a quiet corner and watched them. I never saw a more splendid

scene: the ladies were magnificently dressed; most of them – at least most of the younger ones – looked handsome; but Miss Ingram was certainly the queen.'

* * *

'What aim, what purpose, what ambition in life have you now?'

'My first aim will be to *clean down* (do you comprehend the full force of the expression?) – to *clean down* Moor House from chamber to cellar; my next to rub it with bees-wax, oil, and an indefinite number of cloths, till it glitters again; my third, to arrange every chair, table, bed, carpet, with mathematical precision; afterwards I shall go near to ruin you in coals and peat to keep up good fires in every room; and lastly, the two days preceding that on which your sisters are expected will be devoted by Hannah and me to such a beating of eggs, sorting of currants, grating of spices, compounding of Christmas cakes, chopping up of materials for mince-pies, and solemnising of other culinary rites, as words can convey but an inadequate notion of to the unitiated like you. My purpose, in short, is to have all things in an absolutely perfect state of readiness for Diana and Mary before next Thursdey; and my ambition is to give them a beau-ideal of a welcome when they come.'

* * *

I am afraid the whole of the ensuing week tried his patience. It was Christmas week: we took to no settled employment, but spent it in a sort of merry domestic dissipation. The air of the moors, the freedom of home, the dawn of prosperity, acted on Diana and Mary's spirits like some life-giving elixir: they were gay from morning till noon, and from noon till night. They could always talk; and their discourse, witty, pithy, original, had such charms for me, that I preferred listening to, and sharing in it, to doing anything else. St John did not rebuke

our vivacity; but he escaped from it: he was seldom in the house; his parish was large, the population scattered, and he found daily business in visiting the sick and poor in its different districts.

* * *

'Mr Rochester, if ever I did a good deed in my life – if ever I thought a good thought – if ever I prayed a sincere and blameless prayer – if ever I wished a righteous wish, – I am rewarded now. To be your wife is, for me, to be as happy as I can be on earth.'

'Because you delight in sacrifice.'

'Sacrifice! What do I sacrifice? Famine for food, expectation for content. To be privileged to put my arms round what I value – to press my lips to what I love – to repose on what I trust: is that to make a sacrifice? If so, then certainly I delight in sacrifice.'

Christmas Baptisms in Swaledale

Ten thousand men and a multitude of women and children were baptized in Swaledale on Christmas Day, 627 AD. That is the plain, unbelievable truth, according to the writing of Pope Gregory in his account of the Christianizing of Northumbria.

· A Yorkshire Christmas ·

North-Humbria, remember, stretched from north of the River Humber (Humbria) up to the Scottish border on the Tweed and included all of what we know as Yorkshire. It is odd – not least because Swaledale's lack of communications kept the main flow of history away from it; and though there are strong indications of a Roman presence, and later of Norse settlements, it was only with the arrival of William the Conqueror that the history of Swaledale and Richmond, its beautiful town, was recorded.

Perhaps it was the very remoteness of it that caused the people of the dales to congregate there in safety, the community being protected by the steep fells and fed by the fertile dale. But Bishop Paulinus, who had earlier baptized King Edwin at York, had a missionary zeal about him which he decided to exercise on the Yorkshire pagans hidden in the recesses of Swaledale. About the events leading up to that extraordinary Christmas Day, the Venerable Bede wrote:

> So King Edwin, with all the nobility of his kingdom and a large number of humbler folk accepted the Faith and were washed in the cleansing waters of Baptism in the year of our Lord 627, about 180 years after the first arrival of the English in Britain. The king's baptism took place at York on Easter Day in the church of St Peter the Apostle which the king had hastily built of timber . . .

Indeed, so great was the fervour of faith and desire for baptism among the Northumbrian people that Paulinus is said to have accompanied the king and queen to the royal residence at Ad-Gefrin (Yeavering in Glendale) and remained there thirty-six days constantly occupied in instructing and baptizing. During this period, he did nothing from dawn to dusk but proclaim Christ's saving message to the people, who gathered from all the surrounding villages and countryside;

and when he had instructed them, he washed them in the cleansing waters of Baptism in the nearby River Glen.

'In the province of Deira, Paulinus often stayed with the king, he baptised in the River Swale, which flows near the village of Catterick; for during the infancy of the church in those parts it was not yet possible to build oratories or baptistries.'

Then Pope Gregory, in his writings about Paulinus, amplified the account of what happened on that famous Christmas Day:

> He did regenerate by lively baptism above ten thousand men besides an innumerable multitude of women and children. Having hallowed and blessed the River, called in English 'Swale', he commanded by the voice of criers and masters that the people should enter the river confidently two by two, and in the name of the Trinity baptise one another in turns. And notwithstanding so deep a current and channel, so great and diverse differences of sex and age, not one person took harm.

Christmas comes to Central Stores

HAZEL WHEELER

Once the Standard Fireworks' boxes were out of the way at our Yorkshire village shop, it was time to visit the wholesaler's to buy in for Christmas.

I adored going with mother into town to Beaumont's Warehouse to wander round, after showing our 'pass' proving we had a shop and weren't just the General Public. We selected garishly coloured Chinese Lanterns, fancy paper trimmings, balloons and a few Joy Bombs to put on view at Central Stores. Joy Bombs were rather expensive, some as much as 7s 6d even in the 1930s. I think mother really had herself in mind when she ordered those, but perhaps the butcher, coalman's wife or local doctor might buy one too.

Some were shaped like huge snowmen, with tall black hats set at a rakish angle. I remember one of those cotton wool covered Joy Bombs was a caravan, and we kept it for years, filling it with small new delights year after year.

We preferred them as a centre-piece for the table rather than any posh floral arrangement. It really was the climax of the meal when they were set off and toys, bracelets, necklaces and small Dinky cars flew in all directions.

Lots of boxes of crackers and packs of Christmas cards were ordered too, and all mother had to do was sign for the goods. Dad received the invoice in the post later; mother and I had

the wild spending spree. One Christmas morning I found a huge cardboard box on my bedroom floor. When opened, it revealed a life-size cloth doll, dressed in flimsy mauve dress with matching poke bonnet. I recalled having seen one exactly like it in Beaumont's Warehouse, and I wondered if Father Christmas patronised them from Greenland too.

Writing the cards wasn't a case of shall we or shan't we send any — we racked our brains for more and more people to greet with one. We spread our net wide; it was a pleasure, not a chore, and a whole evening was given over to poring over which to send.

The big wooden kitchen table was extended by winding it open with the handle kept in one of the drawers. My brother Philip and I enjoyed the sensation of sitting at opposite ends while a gap appeared in the table between us. Then the two wooden 'leaves' kept behind the cellar door were brought out and fitted into the space. The only other times the table was extended was when we catered for funeral teas or played table tennis on it.

Once the blinds of the shop were drawn, and business over for the day, the fire was poked into a big blaze and the cards spread out. Our seven cats and Prince, the collie, settled down to snore on the pegged rug and dream of turkey delights to come. Both animals and humans were supremely happy, preparing for the Birth of the New Born King. Oh that animals everywhere could be as loved and secure as they were!

Mother then consulted the long Christmas card list, written in pencil on a piece of white 'cap' paper we used for wrapping bread. Each name ticked off after the correct address had been matched with the same one in the address book.

'Compliments of the Season', mother wrote in her large, sprawling handwriting, dipping her pen into the Stevenson's bottle of ink, time after time. Then 'Love, Hilda, Joe, Hazel and Philip' followed by a row of crosses. What satisfaction

there was in seeing the piles of stamped envelopes waiting on the big sideboard at bedtime.

Next evening after the shop had closed the exciting procedure of extending the table was gone through again. This time for making the decorations. Although some were bought, Philip and I enjoyed gluing those coloured papers together to make chains. Dad stood in the middle of the table with a packet of drawing pins waiting for the paper chains to be carefully handed up.

Drawing pins were hammered lightly into place on the ceiling and picture rails, Chinese lanterns opened out, balloons blown up almost to bursting point. How amazing to see what had been contained in a small flat packet reach such mammoth proportions. Especially those sausage shaped ones which, for a bit of fun, we allowed quickly to expel the air with an aggressively snarling noise which made Prince bark at them and wonder what on earth the world was coming to.

The ball of string kept on the shop counter was brought in to tie firm knots, one of us having to 'just put your finger there' while a knot was tied. We decorated the shop as well, not forgetting strategically placed bunches of mistletoe. Attention was drawn to it for those travellers, passing policemen or customers we liked.

Some customers paid a small sum each week to ease the burden of buying selection boxes and other gift items outright. One huge deep drawer beneath the 'fittings' in the living-kitchen was earmarked solely for Christmas goods 'put by' for customers. Big selection boxes were half a crown in those days I think. Then there were chocolate cigars, with smart jazzy gold papers round their middles, and sweet 'cigarettes' with strawberry pink tips to resemble the lighted end. 'Smokers' Outfits' were very popular – how they would be frowned upon today!

Toy cupboard 'shops' opened out to reveal miniature bottles

filled with Dolly Mixtures and cashews. Tiny celluloid baby dolls with permanently fixed celluloid 'quiffs' over rounded foreheads lay waiting patiently for Christmas Eve. Other favourite stocking fillers were French knitting sets, a wooden reel with four prongs on top, a hook to lift the strands over them, and three or four small balls of brightly coloured mixed shaded wools.

Mother was in her element in the days prior to Christmas. In gleaming white starched overall fresh from the laundry, contrasting with her jet black marcelle waved hair, she looked far more desirable to the commercial travellers than any fairy on top of a tree. They breezed in with flurries of snow through the shop door shouting 'Shop! Merry Christmas everybody', then opened their briefcases out on the counter to tantalise mother with a beautifully wrapped presentation pack of fancy Turkish cigarettes – 'Passing Clouds' was one of the names I

Christmas at Central Stores, Deighton, 1937

recall — or a bottle of perfume in exchange for a 'smacker' beneath the mistletoe. That put the seal on convivial business relationships for the following year.

So many ordinary, un-iced, one-pound Christmas loaves were turned out in our bakehouse that mother couldn't resist giving one to just about everybody in a surge of festive cheer. So each 'rep' had one pushed into his eager hands, and customers who were known to be 'a bit short of the ready' were delighted when mother took yet another from the seemingly endless flow coming into the shop from the bakehouse on big shallow trays.

'I'm sure that tray was full last time I saw it,' Dad frequently remarked in a perplexed voice.

Similarly with the bottles of port, supposedly bought for Christmas Day itself. If any elderly, poor, or simply cold-looking customer entered the shop in the days leading up to Christmas, mother poured them out 'a little tot to warm the cockles of their hearts'.

The final hour before closing on Christmas Eve was hectic. Extra grocery orders to be collected, mothers and dads slipping in to collect presents for children that had been 'put by'. They smuggled them out in brown paper, hoping that children would be too tired to begin rooting into 'the groceries'.

Even the best-kept secrets can go awry. Mrs Cudworth, who had hidden little Audrey's presents at our shop, told us that once Audrey was in bed she had spread them out in the front room ready for filling her daughter's stocking. But Audrey, keyed up with excitement, crept downstairs feeling sick. Realising that everything was on view, her mother without explanation, took off her pinny and flung it over the child's head. Then, guiding her into the kitchen, she administered a spoonful of Fennings Fever Cure and shrouded her head again for the return journey upstairs, muttering some lame excuse about draughts on the way up.

· A Yorkshire Christmas ·

Yes, Christmas Eve was truly magical at our shop. None more so than the year I kept awake long enough actually to hear Father Christmas creeping upstairs. I heard him hiss, in a voice strangely similar to that of John, our shop assistant, 'Are you sure they're asleep yet . . .?', then the growl of a teddy bear rolling on to the floor, and mother giggling somewhere in the distance . . . beyond my dreams. Pure bliss!

Acknowledgements

Friends who have helped me include Nancy and Ernest Tindall of Pickering, Wendy Shaw and Richard Metcalfe, but above all my wife, Nanette, with the illustrations which bear her initials, and typing and improving the manuscript.

All unattributed items are by George Collard, using published and unpublished reference material.

Let Sleeping Vets Lie and *If Only They Could Talk* by James Herriott (Pan Books Ltd); *The Leeds Christmas Book* by P. Brears, Leeds City Museum; *Dickens Christmas Festival at Malton* by Mrs R. Bullimore, Malton Library, and the *Yorkshire Gazette*; *The Diaries of Anne Lister 1791–1840*, Virago Press; *A Christmas Broadcast – Religious Experience* by William Temple (J. Clarke & Co. Ltd); David J. James, Director of Tourism & Amenities of Scarborough Borough Council; Ian Dewhirst, Reference Librarian of Keighley Public Library (City of Bradford); *The Dalesman,* for all its fifty years of articles and information, especially the Christmas 1988 issue; *The Keighley News*; Paul G. Glew, Chairman, Beck Isle Museum.

Picture credits

Bradford Heritage Recording Unit, 137; *P. Brears, Leeds City Museum*, 11, 14, 93; *Ian Dewhirst*, 77, 78; *Halifax Building Society*, 121; *National Railway Museum (W.H. Foster Collection)* 53b, *(Overend 66 Collection)* 53t; *Alan Pickup Collection*, 30, 33, 35, 97, 98, 101, 105; *Nancy Tindall*, 12; *Hazel Wheeler*, 157.